Fredericksburg
History & Biography

Volume 13, 2014

Central Virginia
Battlefields Trust

Central Virginia Battlefields Trust, Inc.
Fredericksburg, Virginia

CENTRAL VIRGINIA BATTLEFIELDS TRUST

Board of Directors
Harriett M. Condon
Lloyd B. Harrison, III
Peter R. Kolakowski
Kevin Leahy
James M. Pates
Josiah P. Rowe, III
Linda P. Wandres
Bradley M. Gottfried
Robert Lee Hodge
Robert K. Krick
Charles G. McDaniel
Eric Powell
Michael P. Stevens
Tom Van Winkle

Executive Director
J. Michael Greenfield

Webmaster
Tom Van Winkle

President……………………………………..……………..Michael P. Stevens
Vice President……………………………….….…………...Harriett M. Condon
Secretary………………………………...…………………………..Robert K. Krick
Treasurer………………………………...…………………Lloyd B. Harrison, III

Editor
Erik F. Nelson

Table of Contents

V   Introductory Notes

9   The Vermont Brigade at Fredericksburg, December 1862.
By Thomas P. Fortune

41   West Wall Soldiers
Researched and compiled by Roy B. Perry, Jr.

103   Minutes of the Common Council of the Town of Fredericksburg, 1864-1865.
Transcribed and annotated by Erik F. Nelson

171   Southern Exposure: Aerial Photo of the Fredericksburg Battlefield.
By Erik F. Nelson

175   Index

Property Acquired by the Central Virginia Battlefields Trust

The CVBT has helped to preserve historic terrain at four major battlefields. Over 1,000 acres of critical ground that would otherwise have been lost to development have been acquired in fee simple (sometimes in partnership with other organizations) or have been placed under an easement. The breakdown, by battlefield, is as follows:

FREDERICKSBURG
Willis Hill
Pelham's Corner
Latimer's Knoll
Braehead
Slaughter Pen Farm

CHANCELLORSVILLE
McLaw's Wedge
Nine Mile Run
Talley Farm
Orange Plank Road
Smith Run
May 1 Field
Flank Attack

WILDERNESS
Grant's Knoll
Wilderness Crossroads

SPOTSYLVANIA COURT HOUSE
Po River/Block House Bridge
Harris Farm

Introductory Notes

This 2014 volume of *Fredericksburg History and Biography* includes historic research, primary source material, and a field examination of Confederate burials with archival follow up. The historic research relates to the study of a brigade of Vermont regiments, veterans of the Peninsular Campaign, who were engaged at Fredericksburg, but not in the main attacks that have since characterized that battle. For primary material, we continue our series on the minutes of the Fredericksburg town council. In the 2012 volume, we covered the period 1860-1861. The 2013 volume continued through the years 1862-1863. This volume takes readers through 1864-1865, concluding the war years and beginning what became a long period of recovery. Finally, a list of soldiers, with brief wartime biographical information, reveals where burials occurred in Fredericksburg during the war. A formal Confederate Cemetery would be established in the war's aftermath, but in the meantime, Fredericksburg found room in its own cemetery for young men far from home.

The following contributors have generously made their work available for this volume:

Thomas P. Fortune is a graduate of Georgetown University, Washington D.C. He resides and practices medicine in Fredericksburg, Virginia. He is a life-long student of American history and a direct descendant of two Civil War soldiers. One was Thomas Fortune, of the 5th Vermont Regiment, and the other was Enoch White, of the 5th California Regiment. Both men were from a little town called Georgia, in Vermont. His article on the Vermont Brigade at the December 1862 battle of Fredericksburg is dedicated to their memory. Tom Fortune lives near the battlefield where the Vermont Brigade proved a solid bulwark against Confederate attacks made in the late afternoon of May 4th, 1863, during the Chancellorsville campaign, but that is another story.

Roy B. Perry, Jr. is the sixth generation of Perrys born in Fredericksburg. His forebears included Robert Oscar Perry, of the 55th Virginia Infantry, who was wounded at Chancellorsville and captured at Falling Waters, after Gettysburg, surviving the war as a prisoner. Another forebear was

James Martin, of the 30th Virginia Infantry, who was killed at Antietam and never recovered for burial at home. Mr. Perry is a member of the Sons of Confederate Veterans, Matthew Fontaine Maury Camp 1722, which has spent considerable time and effort to memorialize the many soldiers who ended up buried in Fredericksburg. He and his group have placed a marker for 51 soldiers in unmarked graves in what was once Potters Field as well as raised, reset, and sometimes replaced individual markers in the Fredericksburg Cemetery, guided by the burial records of the Ladies Memorial Association. His group also placed a marker to memorialize more than 800 casualties sustained by Jubal Early's division on May 4, 1863, at Smith Run in Fredericksburg.

Erik F. Nelson is a graduate of the University of California, Santa Barbara and the editor of this journal. He is the City of Fredericksburg's Senior Planner, but is also the City archivist. His ready access to the original council minutes, including the first drafts that were subsequently copied smooth, has allowed him to provide definitive versions of this material for further research.

Southern Exposure presents an aerial photograph of Fredericksburg taken by the U.S. Army Air Corps on May 15, 1933. The image is from the National Archives, but brought to light by historians at the Fredericksburg and Spotsylvania National Military Park. The Park staff placed the image on line, on their blog called Mysteries and Conundrums (November 13, 2013), where it can be viewed in an interactive mode. It is an exceptionally detailed image and illustrates the scenes described in Tom Fortune's article on the Vermont Brigade.

Erik F. Nelson
Editor

Members of the 6th Vermont at Camp Griffin, Fairfax County, Virginia, Winter of 1861-1862

The Vermont Brigade at Fredericksburg, December 1862

BY THOMAS P. FORTUNE

The role played by the Vermont Brigade at the Battle of Fredericksburg, December 1862, has generally been overlooked by military historians. The futile attacks on Marye's Heights and the lost opportunities of the Federal assaults to the south have understandably dominated accounts of the battle. Closer scrutiny of the Vermonters' role in what has heretofore been considered a quiet sector of the battlefield, however, reveals tactically interesting fighting which was larger in scale, greater in intensity, and longer in duration than has generally been recognized. In addition to these important observations, careful study of the brigade's activities during the Fredericksburg campaign offers insight into the schooling of a quintessentially American fighting unit. On the Virginia peninsula the Vermonter's had stoically endured long marches, poor food, exposure to the elements, sickness, and sometimes slow death. At Lee's Mill, Savage Station, Crampton's Gap and a half dozen other engagements the men had undergone their individual baptisms of fire and experienced firsthand the unimaginable violence of combat. Through the winnowing process of war, commissioned and noncommissioned officers of competence had begun to replace those whose leadership ability fell short. The account of the Vermont Brigade at Fredericksburg is but one chapter in the larger story of how the raw Green Mountain recruits of 1861 became battle hardened veterans.

The "First" or "Old" Vermont Brigade was organized in the fall of 1861. At the beginning of the Fredericksburg campaign the brigade consisted of the 2nd, 3rd, 4th, 5th, and 6th Vermont infantry regiments under the command of Colonel Henry Whiting. The losses in men, clothing, and

Colonel Henry Whiting, Vermont Brigade (photo courtesy of Vermont Historical Society).

equipment incurred during the recent Antietam campaign had mostly been made good by the beginning of November, 1862. At the time of the Fredericksburg battle, the strength of each regiment was between 500 and 600 effectives.[1]

On assuming command of the Army of the Potomac in early November, 1862, Major General Ambrose Burnside organized the corps of his army into three Grand Divisions. Under this scheme the First Corps and the Sixth Corps were grouped together as the Left Grand Division. The Sixth Corps under Major General William F. Smith, former colonel of the 3rd Vermont, consisted of three divisions of three brigades each. Colonel Whiting's Vermonters constituted the Second Brigade of Brigadier General Albion P. Howe's Second Division. Burnside's plan was to put himself between General Robert E. Lee's Confederate army and Richmond by a swift march toward Fredericksburg, followed by a rapid crossing of the Rappahannock River. The pontoon boats required to accomplish the latter part of the operation were late to arrive, however, allowing Lee time to concentrate his army. Fatefully, Burnside decided to test his 115,000-man force against the full might of the Army of Northern Virginia arrayed on the heights behind and to the south of Fredericksburg.

December 10, 1862

On Wednesday, December 10, the Vermont Brigade was camped near Belle Plain, Virginia. The paymaster had arrived, and the sutlers' tents beckoned with a multitude of overpriced goods. Private Peter Abbot, 3rd Vermont, noted that "the sutlers are around pretty thick now, they will take just about

½ of the money [and] some of the boys are just about crazy to spend their money." Unfortunately, extra cash in the pocket was also a temptation to drunkenness and other vices. Colonel Lewis A. Grant of the 5th Vermont saw fit to use the occasion to lecture his men on the "dangerous practice of gambling," a pernicious habit that he "strictly and emphatically prohibited" in his regiment. Realistically, there was little Grant or his fellow colonels could do to permanently curb these amusements. Any merriment attendant upon the paymaster's arrival was short lived, however, as the brigade received orders to march even before all the men had been paid off. The Vermonters were told to prepare for a crossing of the Rappahannock River the next day, which immediately kindled rumors of an approaching battle. That fear was seemingly confirmed when each man was issued 60 rounds of ammunition—40 in the cartridge box, with an extra 20 in the pocket. They also received 3 days cooked rations and were advised to travel light.[2]

The acting brigade commander was 43 year old Colonel Henry Whiting, 2nd Vermont, a graduate of West Point, Class of 1840—a class which included such future luminaries as William T. Sherman and George H. Thomas. At the outbreak of the Civil War, Whiting had been engaged in the lumber business in Michigan; he entered the service as colonel of the 2nd Vermont—the governor's second choice for that position. He never became a popular commander. Among other grievances, the men held it against him that he was not a Vermonter. More seriously, his courage and competence on the battlefield had been called into question. At First Bull Run he had allegedly cowered behind a tree during the thickest of the fight. Eleven months later, at Savage Station, he had ordered the 2nd Vermont to "charge bayonets" while the men were formed in column by division, closed in mass. The regiment stood absolutely motionless in response to this rattled and inapt command. The episode subsequently became a "standing" joke in the brigade. As the senior colonel, Whiting took command of the Vermont Brigade on October 23, 1862, filling the vacancy created when Brigadier General William T. H. Brooks was promoted to head the First Division, Sixth Corps. In December of 1862, Whiting was nursing a grudge over his lack of promotion to Brigadier General—a rank more in keeping with his present responsibilities. Whiting's advancement, however, was not a cause the Vermont authorities were eager to champion.[3]

December 11, 1862

Thursday, December 11, the brigade was ordered up at 4 a.m. The men donned their knapsacks and were on the march by 5 a.m. The ground was frozen hard allowing the artillery and wagons to roll along without impediment. In the distance heavy cannonading could be heard. After a march of 5 miles the brigade arrived at a bend in the Rappahannock River, about a mile south of Fredericksburg.[4]

As the men descended toward the river from Stafford Heights—its brows bristling with artillery, dense clouds of fog filled the valley of the Rappahannock. Army engineers were in the process of throwing two pontoon bridges across the river. The men sheltered under arms on the floodplain, while the Federal artillery fired incessantly over their heads. Rebel skirmishers fired at the engineers but were soon driven off by the Federal guns and their supporting infantry. By 11 a.m. the bridges were completed and passable. At noon the fog finally lifted and a broad flat plain became visible across the river. The Vermonters held their position near the bridges through the afternoon in expectation of being ordered across at a moment's notice. At 4 p.m. General Smith received orders to cross his Sixth Corps. Due to the lateness of the hour, however, he sent only one brigade over to secure a bridgehead on the south side of the river. The remainder of the corps settled down for the night on the north bank.[5]

The Vermonters moved a mile back from the river into a patch of woods. As there was no baggage train on hand, they bivouacked at 10 p.m. without tents or other equipment. The ground was frozen solid, and there was a scattering of lingering snow. Whiting's men had no choice but to spend the night on the uninviting ground. First Lieutenant Erastus Buck, 3rd Vermont, remembered the weather as being very cold, but "we built a good fire and then spread down our overcoats and blinketts *(sic)*, and layed down and rested much better than could be expected."[6]

December 12, 1862

On Friday, December 12, the Green Mountaineers were up at 5 a.m. and moved back down to the river where thousands of other troops were massing. The constant tramp of marching feet, roar of the guns, neighing of horses, and rumble of wagons over the hard ground made an unforgettable impression. At daylight, the Vermont Brigade rapidly crossed the pontoon bridge in a thick fog.[7]

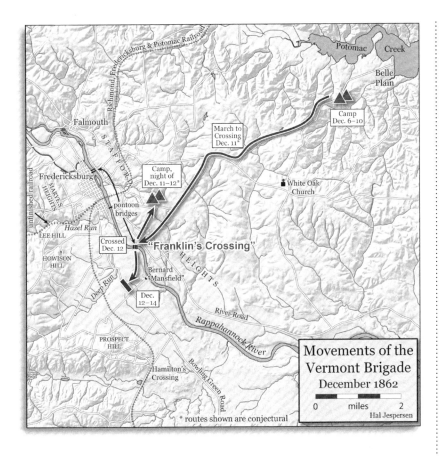

The three divisions of Smith's Sixth Corps crossed the Rappahannock in their numerical order, each in turn climbing a steep 50 foot embankment onto a plateau. General Smith formed the corps 1,200 feet from the river, in a line three brigades deep, parallel to the Bowling Green Road. The First Division (General Brooks) formed on the right, the Second Division (General Howe) took position on the left, and the Third Division (Brigadier General John Newton) remained in columns, in reserve. The left of the Second Division found itself near "Mansfield", the stately Georgian home of Arthur Bernard. In keeping with Smith's overall arrangement, Howe formed his three brigades one behind the other; the Second or Vermont Brigade in the third or rear line. At 10 a.m. the Sixth Corps advanced toward the Bowling Green Road, with each division and its component brigades maintaining their relative positions. Brooks' division crossed Deep Run, taking a position in front of and to the right of that stream. Howe advanced toward a low ridge in front, his right resting on Deep Run. General Newton's division remained in the rear closer to the bridges. General Smith's orders to Brooks and Howe were to hold their positions and avoid any advance that might bring on a general engagement. As the morning fog lifted Howe's and Brooks' movements became visible to the enemy located beyond the railroad.[8]

Between the Bowling Green Road and the railroad—a distance of about 3,000 feet—was a broad, relatively flat, cultivated field, cut in a few places by deep ditches and thick hedges. Howe's area of operation was bounded on the north by Deep Run, a steep ravine choked with new growth timber. On the west, the Richmond, Fredericksburg, and Potomac Railroad ran on mostly level ground with a shallow ditch suitable for defense on either side. The Bowling Green Road ran along the east side of the field. This colonial era thoroughfare was partially sunken with three foot high embankments and broken hedges on both sides. Open fields extended southward between the road and the railroad into the area that would later be occupied by Major General John F. Reynolds' First Corps. The ground rose gradually from the river to a crest located about 300 feet west of the Bowling Green Road. Behind this crest, Howe placed his First Brigade (Brigadier General Calvin E. Pratt) in line of battle with its right resting on Deep Run. Five batteries of artillery occupied the flat ground in Pratt's immediate front, and another battery took position on the right of Deep Run where it could sweep the ravine with canister if necessary. The Third Brigade (Brigadier General Francis L. Vinton), also in line of battle, took position 100 feet behind Pratt, in the Bowling Green Road, its right resting on a sharp bend in Deep Run.[9]

Howe's third line consisted of the Second Brigade (Whiting's Vermonters) formed in close column, by division. In his official report Colonel Whiting described his location as being "in rear of the first ridge after ascending the bluff"—presumably somewhere between the pontoon crossing and the Bowling Green Road. The Vermonters nominally remained in this position for the next two days, a location from which each regiment was called at various times to the division picket line. Due to these heavy commitments, two or more regiments were often on the skirmish line simultaneously. The only permanent occupant of this staging area was the 26th New Jersey, a 9 months regiment assigned to the brigade in September, which saw little action during the battle.[10]

Colonel Nathan Lord, 6th Vermont (photo from Library of Congress).

To the west of Howe's brigade-wide front were a series of low, wooded hills occupied by the enemy. The woods came down to the railroad on the left but receded, as did the hills, to the right. Across the railroad was a field containing the ruins of several small slave cabins. To the right of the cabins, in plain view, was a knoll occupied at times by a rebel battery. On the higher elevations to the right were long range guns which partially enfiladed Howe's position. The Confederates kept up a desultory fire from this direction throughout the day.[11]

Enemy skirmishers posted in the Bowling Green Road had kept up an annoying fire during Howe's preliminary movements. As the general's front line approached the road, the rebel riflemen pulled back. At about this time, the 6th Vermont, under Colonel Nathan Lord, formed the division skirmish line and engaged the retiring Confederates. The 31 year old Lord was the Brigade's only original colonel still in command of a regiment. A Dartmouth graduate and late principal of the Montpelier Academy, Lord still suffered the lingering effects of a bout of dysentery acquired on the Virginia peninsula. The colonel pushed his skirmish line a considerable distance beyond the batteries, which were, at that time, unlimbering in front of the division. As he advanced across the open field, the rebel skirmishers fell back to a point beyond the railroad. Towards evening the 4th Vermont relieved Lord's regiment, and the 6th Vermont returned to the brigade staging area near the Bernard House.[12]

December 13, 1862

Early Saturday morning, December 13, the Third Brigade (Vinton) relieved the First Brigade (Pratt) in the front line. At 6 a.m. General Howe directed Colonel Whiting to send two regiments to the right of the first and second lines respectively. Whiting selected the 3rd and 5th Vermont for this task, but at daylight both regiments were found on the right of the first line of battle, behind a crest, in support of Lieutenant Leonard Martin's battery of rifled guns (F, 5th U.S.). From this position the regiments could be advanced on either side of the run, or directly down the ravine itself as the situation might dictate. The trees bordering Deep Run hid the 3rd Vermont from the rebel guns on the right, sparing it from the shot and shell that would trouble the rest of Howe's division. Soon after these movements, the skirmish line, consisting of the 4th Vermont, became actively engaged. General Vinton (Third Brigade), commanding the front line of Howe's division, dashed to the left where a gap had formed between the 4th Vermont and the skirmishers of the First Corps. At around 9 a.m., Vinton, while attempting to restore the picket line, was shot in the abdomen by a rebel sharpshooter.[13]

As Vinton left the field, the Vermont skirmishers were plagued by canister from the rebel cannons in the field across the railroad. One line of guns was visible along the wood line near the slave cabins, another was observed further back and to the right. Most conspicuous, however, was the battery planted on the knoll in plain sight of the soldiers on the picket line. Its proximity and exposed position made it both dangerous and an attractive target for the Vermont riflemen. The battery appeared to be unsupported except for a line of rebel skirmishers between it and the Green Mountaineers. At 10 a.m. an artillery duel broke out between the rebel guns in front and Howe's artillery. At the height of the clash, two large explosions were heard in the direction of one of the Confederate batteries. A short time after, a Vermont officer came into Captain William McCartney's battery of 12 pounders (A, 1st Massachusetts) carrying a large section of woodwork that had been flung into the skirmish line from an exploded rebel gun carriage. After an exchange of an hour the battery opposed to Captain McCartney's withdrew at a trot, leaving at least one gun and a wrecked limber on the field. A second contest between Howe's artillery and the Confederate guns would take place at 2 p.m. with similar results. Despite the danger, General Howe rode his horse slowly up and down the line, looking out at the fighting.[14]

On Howison's Hill to the right, and partially enfilading Howe's position, the enemy had placed four 3 inch ordnance rifles and ten 10 pound Parrotts. These guns sporadically fired shot and shell in Howe's direction, causing little harm, but pinning his lines of infantry to the cornstubble ground. Two well-entrenched 30 pound Parrotts, on Telegraph and Howison's Hills respectively, hurled heavier ordnance directly at Howe's artillery. Captain Judson Clark (Battery B, 1st New Jersey) recalled that "had these guns continued firing, I think the position held by our line of batteries, could have been untenable." Happily for the Union gunners, the firing from the big rebel guns did not last. Sergeant Ira Dodd, located in the brigade staging area, recalled that "we had to lie flat and be shot at." Describing the special terror of long range shelling, he observed that while few were hit "every catastrophe seems doubly dreadful because you see it all and can do nothing but wonder if it will be your turn next."[15]

At 1 p.m. a reinforced line of rebel skirmishers advanced toward the Federal batteries, and the 2nd Vermont was ordered to check this sudden and unexpected movement. To best meet the threat, Lieutenant Colonel Charles H. Joyce positioned his 2nd Vermont between the already deployed 4th Vermont and Deep Run, the 4th contracting to the left as Joyce's men moved up. The 32 year old Joyce was a lawyer from Northfield, Vermont, who had entered the service with the rank of major. He had played a key role in the ill-will that developed against Colonel Whiting by sending an anonymous letter to the Vermont papers questioning the latter's courage at the first battle of Bull Run. A severe attack of dyspepsia had caused the ambitious Lieutenant Colonel to miss the Battle of Antietam, but for the past two months he had enjoyed good health. Joyce had assumed acting command of the regiment when Whiting took over the brigade.[16]

Lieutenant Colonel Charles H. Joyce, 2nd Vermont Infantry (photo courtesy of Vermont Historical Society).

The 2nd Vermont moved up in line of battle to within 300 feet of the enemy before deploying as a dense line of skirmishers, firing rapidly from the prone position. Dirt flew up in front of the Green Mountaineers as rebel minie balls impacted the sun-softened earth. Private Hiram Tilley had a ball go through his knapsack "and several of the boys had ball holes in their clothing." Tilley fired 48 of his 60 cartridges though "some of the boys fired more than that number." Private Cornelius Nye, of Company D, remembered that "their *(sic)* we laid loading rapidly as possible during the afternoon … with shot and shell flying over our heads from the heights, from our guns to the rebels and from the enemy artillery to ours." Nye reported that 15 of his company were wounded including a man lying only 3 feet away who was shot in the head. Private Storrs Start, of Company H, noted that the regiment was exposed to a "murderous fire of both their artillery and infantry." According to Start, the canister came from a battery of

The Vermont Brigade at Fredericksburg, December 1862

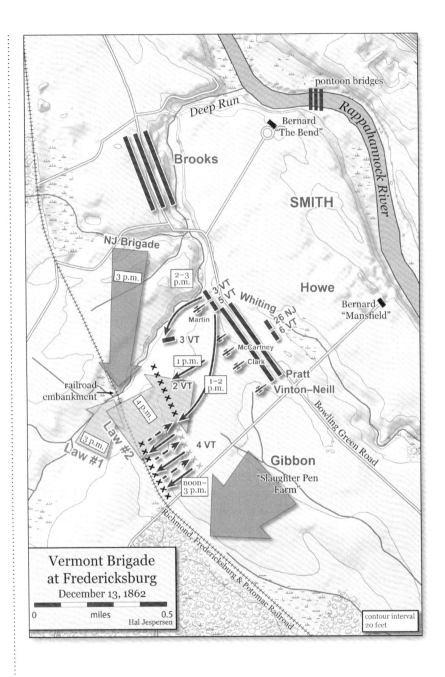

6 guns, in plain view, about 1,400 feet in front of his position. The Federal responded with "about ten pieces of artillery on a little rise of ground in the rear of us firing as lively as possible at the same time." According to Start, "what saved us [was] we were deployed as skirmishers and hugged the ground." From his perch near the Bowling Green Road, Sergeant Dodd could see little of the Vermont skirmishers a half a mile in front "save the puffs of smoke from their rifles." As Dodd gazed toward the action a bullet from the skirmish line struck a soldier standing near him in the chest—killing the man instantly. The sudden movement and return fire of Joyce's men caused the enemy to pull back, although heavy musket firing continued through the afternoon. The 2nd Vermont sustained 65 casualties at Fredericksburg, most of them on the afternoon of December 13.[17]

Lieutenant Colonel George P. Foster, 4th Vermont Infantry (postwar photo, courtesy of Vermont Historical Society).

By the early afternoon Howe's skirmish line consisted of the 4th Vermont on the left and the 2nd Vermont on the right, together covering a front one brigade wide. Thanks to the efforts of the unfortunate General Vinton, the 4th Vermont was now well connected to the skirmishers of Brigadier General John Gibbon's, Second Division, First Corps. The 4th was led by Lieutenant Colonel George P. Foster, a 26 year old lawyer from Walden, Vermont. Foster, a dark haired, nearly six foot tall man of "stalwart proportion", was in temporary command of the regiment, pending the return of Colonel Charles B. Stoughton from sick leave in Vermont. The handsome Lieutenant Colonel, although of "nervous temperament", had capably led his company (G) at the battles of Lee's Mill and Crampton's Gap.[18]

Between noon and 3 p.m. Gibbon's Division advanced to the railroad, across what is today called Slaughter Pen Farm, and was repulsed. The 4th Vermont advanced with Gibbon in order to maintain continuity of the skirmish line. While Gibbon fought at the railroad, Foster's regiment took heavy casualties in an afternoon of intense skirmish fighting. A single canister shot tore through Company B, leaving 2 killed and 14 wounded.

When an exploding shell took down the color bearer, another man promptly took his place. The brass eagle on top of the flag staff was completely shot away, and the regimental colors were so riddled that they scarcely hung together. Some of the men exhausted all their ammunition and had to be resupplied in the field. Private Henry Bush, of Company F, recalled that "the engagement was a hot one for a skirmish fight." Bush, who fired only 39 of his 60 rounds, doubted the accuracy of his marksmanship observing that, "I cannot say I killed a reb, but I saw quite a number of them fall and limp that I fired at."[19]

Captain Stephen M. Pingree, of the 4th Vermont, ordered his 41-man company forward at the start of Gibbon's assault. Company K sprang ahead, with Pingree leading 5 to 6 yards in front. Almost immediately, rebel minie balls began to pepper the ground beneath the Captain's feet. Pingree suppressed a momentary wave of fear and pressed on. While crossing a ditch, Company K received a volley from the Confederate riflemen in front, wounding a number of Pingree's men. As he led the company forward, Pingree glanced to the left where he caught a glimpse of Gibbon's well-ordered ranks, commenting later that "I never saw so magnificent a sight before, but it was sad nevertheless." After advancing 250 feet across the open field, Pingree ordered his men to halt and seek what cover they could. As Company K opened fire on the foe in front, the Captain became so intensely absorbed in his work that he lost track of the bloody events taking place to his left.[20]

Companies G and H of the 4th Vermont, were in the picket reserve. Sergeant William Stevens (Company G) recalled that "the minie balls made constant music over our heads and made an increasing chuck! chuck! chucking in the soft ground among us and we were ordered to hug the turf closely." At that time the regiment was a quarter mile in front of the reserve with an interval of about 5 paces between each man. From his location, Sergeant Stevens watched the advance of Gibbon's Division on the left. Writing home shortly after the battle, he described how "battalion after battalion marched in solid column, with colors waving, towards those woods, so full of death to them, the sight was grand." Soon after this reverie, Stevens' company itself was called to the skirmish line.[21]

Sergeant Marshall Twitchell of Company I, 4th Vermont, remembered crossing a deep ditch as the regiment moved forward. His company occupied a high and exposed position which proved an excellent vantage point from which to witness Gibbon's attack. Years later he wrote that "this useless and grand charge is the most brilliant picture of the war which remains in my mind." Gibbon's division "swept by our left in five lines of battle, its movement as uniform, regular, and precise as they would have been on dress parade." He further noted that there was little firing until Gibbon reached the woods when "there was a long sheet of fire, the division gallantly struggling and advancing against it until all was obscured by smoke." While lying on the ground a bullet passed over Twitchell's left shoulder, cutting a hole through thirteen layers of his rolled rubber blanket. As the 4th Vermont drew back after Gibbon's repulse, Twitchell discovered a man of his company cowering in the ditch they had passed over earlier.[22]

When the 4th Vermont advanced, an opening developed between its right and the left of the 2nd Vermont. Colonel Lewis A. Grant, 5th Vermont, moved his regiment from its position adjacent to Deep Run into the widening gap in the middle of the skirmish line. The 34 year old Grant had been a successful lawyer in Bellows Falls, Vermont before entering the service as the regiment's major. Nicknamed "Aunt Liddy" by his men, he had a reputation for strict adherence to army rules and regulations. Grant had been in command of the regiment at Savage Station on June 29, 1862, when the 5th suffered the greatest loss of any Vermont regiment in the Civil War. On December 13, 1862, he capably moved his regiment forward in the face of intense musket fire, placing his men in the gap between the 2nd and 4th Vermont. Grant's line curved toward the front as it extended to the left in order to establish contact with the 4th Vermont, which by that time was fighting at the railroad. The 5th Vermont became hotly engaged, although its casualties were comparatively light—probably owing to a lull in the activity of the enemy cannons in front. How long the 5th Vermont remained in front is uncertain. Its presence on the skirmish line was probably no longer needed when the 4th Vermont drew back after Gibbon's repulse. Colonel Grant's men probably withdrew a short distance, perhaps all the way back to their original position in support of Martin's Battery, but remained ready to support the other Vermont regiments if needed.[23]

Between 2 and 3 p.m., when the firing in front of the division became general, the 3rd Vermont was ordered from its position in support of Lieutenant Martin's battery to a small crest, approximately 1000 feet in front and close to the skirmish line. The crest was oriented in such a way that a body of men hunkered down behind it could deliver a surprise raking fire into an enemy line of battle advancing across the field toward Howe's

Colonel Breed N. Hyde, 3rd Vermont Infantry (photo from Library of Congress).

front line. The safest way forward was to move directly up the ravine of Deep Run, conveniently located on the regiment's immediate right. By this means, the men would be protected from the canister and rifle fire of the enemy, as well as the shells of their own guns flying overhead. Upon receipt of these orders, Colonel Breed N. Hyde, 3rd Vermont, inexplicably hesitated and allowed his second in command, Lieutenant Colonel Thomas O. Seaver, to take the regiment forward.[24]

Hyde was a 30 year old merchant from Hyde Park, Vermont. He had attended West Point for two years before being dismissed in 1853 for academic deficiency. The men of the 3rd Vermont did not hold Colonel Hyde in high esteem, one member of the regiment noting that "our pompous colonel was a better camp ornament than fighting soldier." Seaver was a 29 year old apprentice lawyer from Woodstock, Vermont. Blind in the left eye from a childhood accident, he had attended Norwich University in Vermont for two years where he received some basic military training. He had entered the service as Captain of Company F and distinguished himself at the Battle of Lee's Mill on April 16, 1862. Hyde and Seaver had locked horns over regimental promotions in September of 1862. During the colonel's absence, Seaver had forwarded a slate of candidates at odds with Hyde's own choices. In a letter to the Vermont Adjutant and Inspector General, Hyde protested that Seaver had acted out of personal animosity and harbored an "extreme love of command." Whatever the merits of this claim, the situation on December 13, 1862 called for immediate action.[25]

Lieutenant Colonel Seaver called the regiment to attention, ordered it to right face, and filed the men into the ravine. He then moved the regiment through the steep, timber-clogged valley of Deep Run, the men moving with great care to keep out of sight of the enemy. After working their way upstream a fifth of a mile, the Vermonters reached a point near the designated crest. Both Lieutenant Colonel Seaver and Major Samuel E. Pingree asked Hyde to deploy the regiment, but the colonel seemed paralyzed by fear. Private Charles Dubois, of Company G, remembered that Colonel Hyde "crouched behind some of the men with terror stamped in every feature, some of the boys told him to get out of the way or they would kick him out."

After a tense few moments, Seaver assumed command and ordered the regiment to file out of the ravine, left in front. The men crawled up out of the gully through some tall weeds and dry grass; they then formed in line of battle behind the low ridge and lay flat on the ground. A surgeon and hospital force remained in the ravine, ready to receive the wounded. During these movements, Private Dubois noticed that Colonel Hyde had "slunk off into the ravine out of sight." In their advanced position, a mere 20 feet behind the division skirmish line, the men of the 3rd Vermont observed the work of the riflemen in front, and awaited further developments.[26]

Lieutenant Colonel Thomas O. Seaver, 3rd Vermont Infantry (photo courtesy of Vermont Historical Society).

About 3 p.m. the New Jersey Brigade of Brook's First Division, Sixth Corps, received orders to drive the enemy from an embankment located where the railroad crossed Deep Run. Advancing diagonally from north of the run, the Jerseymen enjoyed initial success, but were driven back by a determined enemy counterattack. Corporal James Clarke, of the 3rd Vermont, watched from behind the crest as the rebels charged on two or three New Jersey regiments and "routed them and drove them back like a flock of sheep." Flush with this success, the rebels—mostly from the 54th and 57th North Carolina of Brigadier General Evander Law's brigade–advanced on Howe's first line. According to General Law, the North Carolinians came to within 300 yards of the Bowling Green Road, a short distance from the Union batteries. Captain William McCartney (Battery A, 1st Massachusetts) watched the Vermont skirmishers fall back "in perfect order, fighting coolly and gallantly." McCartney opened fire on the charging Confederates with solid shot, the captain "not deeming it prudent to use either shell or case shot over the skirmishers." As a last precaution, McCartney "caused two rounds of canister to be placed at the muzzle of the guns"—he regretted not having the opportunity to use it.[27]

The 3rd Vermont had been lying undetected behind the small crest adjacent to Deep Run for nearly an hour, when Law's North Carolinians charged toward the Bowling Green Road. Upon hearing the rebels' "peculiar yell," the Green Mountaineers warily craned their heads over the crest. They were quickly spotted by the approaching Confederates, who turned toward the crouching Vermonters and opened fire. In short order, there were five fresh casualties for the ambulance men. Lieutenant Colonel Seaver waited until the enemy was only 150 feet from his position, when he ordered the men to rise and fire. Private Dubois recalled that "we jumped to our feet and gave them a withering volley which caused many of them to bite the dust." According to First Lieutenant Erastus Buck the men "rose up and fired a terrific volley into them and gave a yell and charged on them and drove them in all directions and confusion." Corporal Clarke noted that after the first volley, the rebels "turned and run as fast the other way as they was running this way." Before Law's men got out of range, Clarke continued, "we gave them about three volleys more which made quite a number of gray spots on the ground, near where they turned." The satisfied corporal later confessed that "it done me a great deal of good to see them running back."[28]

In their impetuous advance, the North Carolinians had failed to appreciate that Federal troops might be waiting in ambush along Deep Run. The sudden appearance of the 3rd Vermont on their left flank, together with the fire from the Federal infantry and artillery in front, was enough to send the rebels reeling back toward the railroad. Captain McCartney noted that the rebels in front of his battery "broke ranks and withdrew in considerable confusion and with much celerity." According to a member of the 26th New Jersey, some of the Confederates willingly surrendered, "declaring themselves to be tired of the war, and their intention of serving no longer."[29]

After Law's men retired, the 3rd Vermont remained in its advanced position until the next morning. Lieutenant Colonel Seaver sent out Company H to screen the regiment from any probing activity by the enemy along

> Private Dubois remembered a North Carolina soldier, who had been shot in both legs, calling to his friends for help. As the night hours passed and hope of rescue faded, the soldier's patient pleas turned to bitter curses against his comrades, his state, and the Confederacy.

Deep Run. Company H advanced toward the railroad and joined with the skirmishers of the 2nd and 4th Vermont, already on duty in front. During the night, the rebels advanced a skirmish line close to the Vermont riflemen in an attempt to rescue some of their wounded. The rattling of their equipment gave the movement away, and a volley from the Vermonters drove the rebels back into the ditches along the railroad. Soon after, Seaver's men began to hear the cries of the wounded located between the opposing skirmish lines. Private Dubois remembered a North Carolina soldier, who had been shot in both legs, calling to his friends for help. As the night hours passed and hope of rescue faded, the soldier's patient pleas turned to bitter curses against his comrades, his state, and the Confederacy.[30]

Close of day, December 13, found the 2nd and 4th Vermont on the skirmish line in front of General Howe's division. The 3rd Vermont was a few hundred feet away, at the spot next to Deep Run where they had surprised the North Carolinians. Colonel Grant's 5th Vermont was also nearby, although its exact position in the late afternoon is uncertain. The successive deployment of the Vermont regiments on December 13 proved effective in shielding the Second Division from probing attacks by the enemy's skirmishers and in repulsing General Law's line of battle in the late afternoon. A feature of the December 13 fighting was the mixing of loose skirmish formations with standard linear tactics. For example, when the 2nd Vermont went forward in the early afternoon, it did so in a traditional line of battle. At the limit of its advance, however, it broke up into a loose, flexible line of riflemen. Similarly, while the 3rd Vermont advanced up Deep Run and deployed behind the crest using cover and concealment, it delivered a timed volley, and bounded onto the field in linear formation. These improvised tactical experiments show an army struggling to find a style of combat that responded to conditions in the field, as well as to the accuracy of the standard issue rifled firearms.[31]

December 14, 1862

At early dawn, December 14, the Vermont Brigade relieved the Third Brigade (Brigadier General Thomas H. Neil) in the front line. For Lieutenant Colonel Joyce's 2nd Vermont and Lieutenant Colonel Foster's 4th Vermont this simply meant withdrawing a few hundred feet from the skirmish line. The latter two regiments, together with the 26th New Jersey, formed in line of battle in the sunken Bowling Green Road. Colonel Hyde's

3rd Vermont returned to the support of Martin's Battery (F, 5th U.S.) next to Deep Run. Because the fog had burned off early, the Vermonters made these movements under a harassing fire from the enemy pickets.[32]

The 5th and 6th Vermont, under Colonels Grant and Lord respectively, were back on the skirmish line, actively engaged with the enemy for most of the day. The 6th Vermont had missed the fight of December 13, having been in the rear, along with the 26th New Jersey, as part of General Howe's third line. For some reason, the bulk of the fighting on December 14 fell to the 5th Vermont, which had a total of 13 men killed and wounded, compared to the 6th Vermont's total of just 1 killed. The nature of the fighting on December 14 was similar to that experienced by the Vermonters on the previous day. Private John Pitridge, of the 5th Vermont, wrote home shortly after the battle that "we had orders to keep down so we wouldn't get hit." Having wisely heeded these instructions, Pitridge felt shot, shell, and minie balls pass uncomfortably close to him as he "lay flat on the sand." He further noted that "all we could hear was 'Boom, Bang, Whiz' then 'Slap' into the dirt by your side - if it didn't hit you or someone else." So it went for two long hours while "the rebels and our men was *(sic)* playing with their iron barrels." While tending to his portion of the skirmish line, Colonel Grant was hit in the left thigh by a spent musket ball. The wound, while painful, was not life threatening, and "Aunt Liddy" remained on duty with the regiment.[33]

Late in the evening, a Confederate flag of truce, to allow for the removal of the dead and wounded, appeared in front of the division. Firing ceased almost immediately, and within 15 minutes Private Pitridge was shaking hands with the very men who had been eagerly trying to kill him only moments before. Private Lester Hack remembered that after sunset, when the firing had ceased, the men of Company F and their rebel counterparts began to talk:

> They said they would not fire if we would not—we agreed—Met them half way and shook hands with them and had a good talk … they parted hoping to meet again under beter (sic) circumstances— I realy (sic) believe this thing will never be settled by fighting.

At night the men lay on their arms, fortunate that the weather had become unseasonably warm.[34]

December 15–18, 1862

At 5 a.m. on Monday, December 15, the Third Division (Newton) relieved Howe's three brigades of infantry. The Vermonters marched out of the Bowling Green Road by their right flank, and took position near the pontoon bridges. After four days of constant marching and fighting, the Green Mountaineers were ready for some rest. Auspiciously, the day was warm and the enemy guns silent. During the afternoon, the sick and wounded were evacuated over the bridges. At 6 p.m., after the Vermonters had prepared their bedding for the night, orders came to "fall in." Three hours later, the Vermont Brigade crossed to the north side of the Rappahannock and camped in a piece of woods on Stafford Heights. Sergeant William Stevens, 4th Vermont, remembered that "when the order to 'fall in rapidly' came in I could not believe we were to retreat, but other orders and our direction of march soon taught us the truth." Private George Mellish, 6th Vermont, wrote home in disgust that "after having been across four days fooling around and getting a lot of men killed and doing no good we crossed the bridge on the night of the 15th, took up the bridge and now occupy this side of the river."[35]

After a cold, windy, and rainy night the Vermonters awoke to find themselves and their gear soaking wet. A soldier of the 6th Vermont observed the rebels across the river scouring the plain where the brigade had been deployed on the preceding days. From Stafford Heights the men could see the devastated town of Fredericksburg about a mile to their right, one soldier noting its "almost demolished" condition. On Wednesday, December 17, the brigade moved a mile further back from the river. There they were met by a hoard of sutlers hawking their wares. On Thursday, December 18, the Green Mountaineers concluded the Fredericksburg campaign by marching 5 miles back to their previous camp near Belle Plain.[36]

Aftermath

The union army lost over 12,000 killed, wounded, and missing at the Battle of Fredericksburg. Compared to the losses of Reynold's Corps or those suffered in front of Marye's Heights, the casualties in the Vermont Brigade were light, totaling 144. Most of these losses were sustained by the 2nd and 4th Vermont on December 13, while engaged in intense skirmish fighting and subject to heavy canister fire. The casualties would have been much higher if the Vermonters had fought in line of battle, but because they were deployed as skirmishers and remained flat on the ground for hours at a time, the Green Mountaineers escaped the slaughter endured by the Federal troops on their right and left. Howe's division was said to have been in a quiet sector of the field, a sentiment that would have puzzled the Vermont soldiers who had just lived through four days of the most intense fighting some of them had ever seen.[37]

Three quarters of the wounded in Howe's Division were Vermonters. The Battle of Fredericksburg had been the first test of Medical Director Jonathan Letterman's October 1862 reorganization of the Army of the Potomac's medical department. In previous battles the care of the wounded had been haphazard and disorganized, leading to unnecessary suffering and death. The hospital team that accompanied the 3rd Vermont up Deep Run on December 13 is a good example of Letterman's new system of forward triage. When Lieutenant Colonel Seaver led the regiment to its advanced position adjacent to the run, a medical officer, nurse, and hospital orderly followed close behind. Sheltered in the ravine, these three men established a temporary depot to provide emergency care to the regiment's wounded. Stretcher bearers probably carried the more serious cases back down the ravine to ambulances waiting near the Bowling Green Road. Similar arrangements for the care of the wounded had been adopted in the other Vermont regiments and throughout the army. From the Bowling Green Road, the ambulances would have transported the injured to the Second Division hospital located at Arthur Bernard's "Mansfield." Here, a team of three surgeons, chosen from among the best in the division, performed any necessary amputations. On the afternoon of December 15, all the wounded were successfully evacuated across the three pontoon bridges to a field hospital located behind Stafford Heights.[38]

The troubled tenure of Colonel Henry Whiting as brigade commander did not long survive the Fredericksburg battle. Whiting's brief after action report—vague and confusing in key respects—has the flavor of a second hand document rather than one prepared by an active participant. The Colonel is conspicuous by his absence from the Vermont primary source material detailing the fighting of December 12 through 14. It surely would not have escaped the Vermonters' notice that, on the morning of December 13, it was General Vinton (Third Brigade) rather than Colonel Whiting who was grievously wounded along the skirmish line. For all these reasons,

Captain Stephen M. Pingree's observations concerning Whiting's behavior during the late battle probably contain more than a hint of truth:

> *Henry Whiting—the <u>hero</u> of Bull Run, Savage Station, and Fredericksburg—formerly Col. 2nd Vermont … was a graceless coward at Fredericksburg—and from this (which I know) I feel justified in presuming the truth of similar reports of his conduct at the first Bull Run. He has been in command of our Brigade every day since Nov. 19, except <u>Dec 13 &14</u>!! On the 13th he was 1 ½ miles from the attacking line (2nd and 4th Rgts.) and ought to have been tried for cowardice.*

With his reputation further damaged and no promotion in sight, Whiting resigned from the service on February 9, 1863. Lieutenant Chester K. Leach, 2nd Vermont, correctly surmised the reason for Whiting's departure, and in language direct and colorful wrote that, "Colonel Whiting I understand has tendered his resignation—and the reason for it is I believe that the Eagle that sits on his shoulder cannot be made to shit a Star." The ranking colonel, Lewis A. Grant, of the 5th Vermont, succeeded the unfortunate Whiting as brigade commander.[39]

Other important leadership changes took place in the brigade at this time. Lieutenant Colonel Joyce had skillfully and bravely led the 2nd Vermont during the recent battle. General Howe had singled out the well-liked Joyce for special praise in his after action report, and his promotion to regimental command would have been a foregone conclusion. Within days of the battle, however, a severe bout of recurrent dyspepsia felled the otherwise vigorous lieutenant colonel, which led to his resignation on January 8, 1863. Colonel Hyde, of the 3rd Vermont, faced a court martial for his egregious failure of leadership along Deep Run. The hesitation and paralysis of action he demonstrated on December 13 clearly disqualified him from further command. Probably fatal to Hyde's cause, however, was a notable lack of support from within the regiment. A sergeant of the 3rd Vermont, himself neutral with respect to the colonel's case, observed that "there is a very bitter spirit between some of the officers of the regiment and him [Hyde], and they will leave no stone unturned in their attempt to break him." Colonel Hyde claimed he had been prostrated by diarrhea, but resigned to prevent dismissal for cowardice. The popular and battle-tested Lieutenant Colonel Seaver replaced Hyde as colonel of the 3rd Vermont on January 15, 1863.

Colonel Nathan Lord, although debilitated by dysentery, had capably led the 6th Vermont while over the river. The colonel's health completely broke down after the battle, however, forcing him to resign on December 18, 1862 —the day the regiment returned to its camp at Belle Plain.[40]

Immediate reactions to the Federal defeat at Fredericksburg were angry. "What a finale to Burnside's grand advance!" fumed Sergeant William Stevens, 4th Vermont. "Viewed as a subject for history," he continued, "Saturday's sights were sublime; as a blunder of generals it was— search Webster's [dictionary] for 'fail' for the proper word!" Colonel Lewis A. Grant, 5th Vermont, tried to put the best face on the army's demoralizing defeat. In a letter published in the Burlington Free Press dated December 17, Grant noted that "the great 5 days Battle of Fredericksburg is now over." Somewhat speciously he added that "it has proved a failure to our arms– not a defeat, but a failure." Some newspapers took a similar line, attempting to gloss over the thrashing Burnside's army had received. Private Thomas Murphy, of the 6th Vermont, however, was not fooled by the rosy journalistic spin, noting in his diary that "the papers are trying to cover our late defeat by calling it a reconnaissance in force, which is all humbug." By the end of December the casualty lists and Burnside's official report had been published in the papers, completely undermining any optimistic pretense. When the magnitude of the army's defeat became known, a deep melancholy set in among the Vermonters. Chaplain Edward P. Stone, 6th Vermont, dejectedly observed that he "never saw the men and officers so depressed except at Harrison's Landing and for my own part I cannot see anything human to encourage them." By New Year's Eve, spirits had begun to revive somewhat. Seated in the relative comfort of his log hut near White Oak Church, the brigade's winter encampment, Private Edson Emery, 2nd Vermont, jotted in his diary that "another year in the service has passed" and noted that he felt blessed that "our loss in battle has been small as we have been in slight engagements." Emery was referring to the losses of the Vermont Brigade which had been comparatively light at the recent titanic clashes of Antietam and Fredericksburg. Little could he know, however, that over the next two and a half years the Vermonters would participate in some of the bloodiest fighting of the Civil War and compile a casualty list that would not be exceeded by any other Union brigade during the war.[41]

❧ NOTES ❧

1. George Grenville Benedict, *Vermont in the Civil War A History of the Part Taken by the Vermont Soldiers and Sailors in the War For the Union,* 2 volumes (Burlington: The Free Press Association, 1886) 1:235-236 [Benedict]; Report *of the Adjutant and Inspector General of the State of Vermont from November 1, 1862 to October 1, 1863* (Montpelier: Walton's Steam Printing, 1863) 14-22. There were two all-Vermont brigades: the "First" discussed here, and a "Second" composed of 9 months troops whose only action was at Gettysburg. The number of men on duty with each regiment on 1 January 1863 was: 727 - 2nd; 573 – 3rd, 457 – 4th, 457 – 5th, 546 – 6th. The 26th New Jersey, a nine months regiment, was attached to the Vermont brigade at this time. It saw little action at first Fredericksburg. Some primary source material from the unit has been used to round out this account.

2. Solomon Heaton to Parents, 10 December 1862, Special Collections, University of Vermont Library [UVt]; Peter M. Abbot to unknown correspondent, 13 December 1862, Peter M. Abbott Civil War Letters, MSS-17 #2, Vermont Historical Society [VHS]; General Order No. 61, Order Book 5th Vermont Volunteers, Records of the Adjutant General's Office, Records Group 94, National Archives [RG 94]; Chester K. Leach to wife, 10 December 1862, UVt; Hiram Tilley to parents, 15 December 1862, Bound Manuscripts–vol. 323, Fredericksburg and Spotsylvania National Military Park [FSNMP]; Thomas Murphy diary, 10 December 1862 entry, The Civil War Papers of Thomas Parish Murphy, Misc 955, VHS; Edward Stone to father, 9 December 1862, Edward P. Stone Letters, MSS-25 #72, VHS; Stephen Pingree to Cousin Augustus, 10 December 1862, Pingree/Hunton/Stickney Papers, Doc 382, VHS.

3. George Cullum, *Biographical Register of Officers and Graduates of the United States Military Academy*, 2 volumes (New York: D. Van Nostrand, 1862) 2: 44, entry 1033; "Letter to the Editor" dated 11 August 1861 in *Vermont Freeman*, 20 August 1861; James H. Walbridge to George G. Benedict, 8 February 1884, Carton 2, Benedict Family Papers, UVt; Henry Whiting to Lieutenant E. Mattocks, 2 February 1863, Volunteer Service Records of Henry Whiting, RG 94. Vermont Governor Erastus Fairbanks first offered command of the 2nd Vermont to Colonel Israel B. Richardson. The latter was a Vermont native,

graduate of West Point, and a veteran of the Mexican War. An alternate version of the Bull Run story had Colonel Whiting hiding behind a boulder.

4. "From the 26th Regiment, Battlefield of Fredericksburg", *Newark Daily Mercury*, 18 December 1862; *War of the Rebellion: A Compilation of the Official Records of the Union and Confederate Armies*, 128 volumes (Washington: U.S. Government Printing Office, 1880-1901) Series 1, Volume XXI [OR], 448; George T. Stevens, *Three Years in The Sixth Corps* (New York: D. Van Nostrand, 1867) 166-167 [Stevens]; Murphy diary, 11 December 1862 entry; Abbott letter, 13 December 1862. One source (Murphy) says the march was 7 miles. The cannonading heard during the march was probably the targeted shelling of the Confederate infantry along the Rappahannock, which was contesting the laying of the upper and middle pontoon bridges at Fredericksburg.

5. "The Vermont Soldiers in the Battle at Fredericksburg", *Rutland Herald*, 25 December 1862 ["Vermont at Fredericksburg"]; George Mellish to parents, 18 December 1862, Huntington Library, San Marino, California; Erastus Buck to wife, 15 December 1862 in *Buck's Book*, J.E. Balzer editor (Bolingbrook, Illinois: Balzer and Associates, 1993) 60-62; Stevens, 166; Benedict, 341; OR, 448, 523. The union official reports generally refer to the Stafford side of the river as "north" and the Fredericksburg/Spotsylvania side as "south" and that practice is followed here. Beginning at noon on December 11, 1862 the general bombardment of Fredericksburg began. It is curious that none of the Vermont primary sources cited herein refer to that event. A third pontoon bridge at the lower crossing was added on December 12; all three bridges were taken up on December 15.

6. Buck letter, 15 December 1862; "Vermont at Fredericksburg"; Abbott letter, 13 December 1862; Murphy diary, 11 December 1862 entry. The temperature at Washington, D.C. at 9 p.m. on 11 December was 32.5°; at 7 a.m. on 12 December it was 21°. See Robert K. Krick, *Civil War Weather in Virginia* (Tuscaloosa: The University of Alabama Press, 2007) 80.

7. Stevens, 169; OR, 449; *Carpetbagger From Vermont, the Autobiography of Marshall Harvey Twitchell*, Ted Tunnell editor (Baton Rouge: Louisiana State University, 1989) 49 [Twitchell Autobiography].

8. OR, 523, 526, 529, 532-533, 535; Troop Movement Map (2001)–Fredericksburg, 13 December 1862, 5 sheets, FSNMP; Benedict, 341; Lewis A. Grant to George G. Benedict, 4 January 1884, Benedict Family Papers, UVt; "From the 26th Regiment, Battlefield of Fredericksburg", *Newark Daily Mercury*, 18 December 1862.
9. OR, 449, 525, 529-533; *Supplement to the Official Records of the Union and Confederate Armies*, 100 volumes (Wilmington: Broadfoot Publishing Company, 1994) Part 1, Volume 3 [Supplement], 799; Lewis A. Grant letter, 4 January 1884; Evander Law to Edward P. Alexander, 15 October 1866, Southern Historical Collection, Wilson Library, University of North Carolina, Chapel Hill. The bluff at the lower pontoon crossing has an elevation of 50 feet—from there, the ground gradually rises another 30 feet to a ridge, parallel to and about 300 feet west of the Bowling Green Road. The ridge is more pronounced on the right, where the road climbs out of Deep Run; further to the left it is less distinct. Unfortunately, modern development has destroyed any topographic subtleties. The precise location of Howe's first line is uncertain, an educated guess would be 100 feet west of the Bowling Green Road on the reverse slope of the aforementioned ridge. Later in the battle, the first line was located in the road. There is an excellent aerial view of Fredericksburg taken in 1933 that includes Howe's entire area of operation at: *http://npsfrsp.files.wordpress.com/2013/11/1933-aerial-frsp-rg-18aa-box-128-smaller1.jpg*
10. OR, 532; Supplement, 792. In his official report Whiting does not say that his brigade moved forward with the rest of the division at 10 a.m., possibly this movement was accomplished by the First (Pratt) and Third (Vinton) Brigades only.
11. OR, 525, 533; Benedict, 341; Lewis A. Grant letter, 4 January 1884. The area where these structures stood is today referred to as "Bernard's Cabins". The Bernard's Cabins area and the nearby knoll were occupied by the Confederate batteries of Captains Greenlee Davidson and Joseph Latimer respectively during the battle of 13 December. The knoll is today known as "Latimer's Knoll" after the eponymous captain.
12. OR, 530, 532, 668; Supplement, 793; Elisha Barney diary, 12 December 1862 entry, Records of the Vermont Civil War Centennial Commission, microfilm series PRA 356, Reel 2847, Public Records Division, Middlesex, Vermont; George Mellish letter, 18

December 1862; Murphy diary, 12 December 1862 entry; Tilley letter, 15 December 1862; Benedict, 209. Three companies of the 6th Vermont (C, E, and H) formed the picket reserve (Mellish letter). The 2nd Vermont may have been on the skirmish line for a time on 12 December, the sources are conflicting.

13. OR, 524-525, 530, 532-533; Troop Movement Map (2001)—Fredericksburg, 13 December 1862, Sheet 5: 3:00 P.M.–5:00 P.M., FSNMP; Supplement, 760; "Vermont at Fredericksburg"; Civil War Memoir of Charles Dubois, 189, UVt; Stevens, 171. After Vinton's wounding, command of the Third Brigade devolved on Brigadier General Thomas H. Neil. General Vinton survived his injury and lived until 1879. The First Corps skirmishers were from the 13th Massachusetts.

14. OR, 525, 530, 668; Supplement, 783; William DeLoss Love, *Wisconsin in the War of the Rebellion* (Chicago: Church and Goodman, 1865) 346. The number of rounds fired by the batteries in front of Howe's Division during the battle was as follows: Kidd, (B) 1st Maryland—315; Butler, (G) 2nd United States—796 (13 December only); McCartney, (A) 1st Massachusetts—not stated; Clark, (B) 1st New Jersey–386; Martin, (F) 5th United States—626 (see Supplement, reports of respective battery commanders).

15. OR, 578, 587; Supplement, 755, 782-783; Murphy diary, 13 December 1862 entry; Ira S. Dodd, *The Song of the Rappahannock* (New York: Dodd, Mead and Company) 78. Both 30 pound Parrotts exploded during the course of the engagement, ending this threat to Howe's batteries. After the Fredericksburg battle, Telegraph Hill became known as Lee's Hill.

16. OR, 530, 533; Edson Emery diary, 13 December 1862 entry, Civil War Miscellaneous Collection, United States Military History Institute, Carlisle, Pennsylvania; Jacob G. Ullery, *Men of Vermont: Biographical History of Vermonters* (Brattleboro: Transcript Publishing Company, 1894) 228; "Letter to editor" dated 11 August 1861 in *Vermont Freeman*, 20 August 1861; "Affidavit of James H. Walbridge", 9 March 1887, Pension Records of Charles H. Joyce, RG 94; Tilley letter, 15 December 1862.

17. Hiram Tilley to parents, 15 December 1862, Bound Manuscripts–vol. 323, FSNMP; Cornelius Nye to unknown correspondent, undated,

Sylvanus Nye Papers, MS 39, VHS; Storrs W. Start to friend Thomas, 4 March 1863, Bound Manuscripts - vol. 229, FSNMP; Chester K. Leach to wife, 16 December 1862, UVt; *The Song of the Rappahannock*, 79-80; OR, 141. General Howe is mistaken in stating that the 2nd Vermont went forward early on Saturday morning 13 December (OR, 530). Colonel Whiting (OR, 533) fixes the time of Joyce's advance as 1 p.m., while Private Emery (13 December diary entry) places it at 1:30 p.m.

18. Roger D. Hunt and Jack R. Brown, *Brevet Brigadier Generals in Blue* (Gaithersburg: Olde Soldier Books, 1996) 211; Volunteer Service and Pension Records of George P. Foster, RG94 ["nervous temperament"]; Volunteer Service Records of Charles B. Stoughton, RG 94; Benedict, 168 ["stalwart proportion"].

19. OR, 141; Benedict, 345; "Report of Colonel Charles B. Stoughton, Fourth Regiment", *Report of the Adjutant and Inspector General of the State of Vermont from November 1, 1862 to October 1, 1863,* 73; Henry J. Bush to father and mother, 16 December 1862, Bound Manuscripts-vol. 36, FSNMP.

20. Stephen M. Pingree to Cousin Albert, 23 April 1863, VHS.

21. William B. Stevens to sister, 22 December 1862, Robinson Family Papers, Rokeby Museum, Sheldon, Vermont.

22. Twitchell Autobiography.

23. Lewis A. Grant letter, 4 January 1884; "Major-General Lewis Addison Grant", *The Vermonter*, Vol. 32 (1927), No. 3, 45; "Colonel Grant to Adjutant General Washburn, 17 December 1862" in *Burlington (Daily) Free Press*, 26 December 1862.

24. "Vermont at Fredericksburg"; Benedict, 128-129; Undated note of George G. Benedict titled "1st Brigade, December 13, 1862", Carton 7, Benedict Family Papers, UVt.

25. "Report of the Progress, Aptitude, and Habits of Certain Cadets of the United States Military Academy", 25 June 1853, Records of the Inspector USMA, RG 94; Dubois Memoir, 190, UVt ["pompous … soldier"]; "Colonel Thomas O. Seaver", *Vermont Standard*, 18 July 1912; Grenville M. Dodge and William Arba Ellis, *Norwich University 1819-1911 Her History, Her Graduates, Her Roll of Honor*, 3 volumes (Montpelier: The Capitol City Press, 1911) 2: 622; Pension Record of Thomas O. Seaver, RG 94; B. N. Hyde letter, 20 September 1862 in Correspondence 3rd Vermont Volunteers, Records of the Adjutant

and Inspector General, microfilm series PRA 364, reel F26019, Public Records Division, Middlesex, Vermont ["extreme love of command"]. Colonel Hyde missed the Battle of Antietam, returning to duty on the day after the battle concluded. Hyde's timely absence raised the eyebrows of Major Samuel E. Pingree, 3rd Vermont (Samuel E. Pingree to Cousin Hunton, 10 October 1862, VHS). Norwich University was the only private military college located in the north during the war. Founded in 1819 by former West Point superintendent Alden Partridge, the Norwich curriculum was created in opposition to the reforms instituted by Sylvanus Thayer at the U.S. Military Academy. Partridge feared the rise of an aristocratic officer class, and extolled the virtues of the well-educated citizen soldier. Hundreds of Norwich alumni served in the Federal army during the Civil War.

26. Benedict, 344; "Vermont at Fredericksburg"; Benedict—Undated note; Abbott letter, 15 December 1862; "From the 26th Regiment, Camp Near King George Courthouse", *Newark Daily Mercury*, 27 December 1862; Buck letter, 15 December 1862; Dubois Memoir, 190; James Clarke to mother, 24 December 1862, Bound Manuscripts—vol. 489, FSNMP. Benedict (Undated note) gives as authority for Hyde's "hesitation" and "paralysis by fear" verbal statements to him by Lieutenant Colonel Seaver and Major Samuel E. Pingree. The latter was a 30 year old Dartmouth graduate and lawyer from Hartford, Vermont. He had entered the service as Lieutenant in Company I, but was soon promoted to Captain. At Lee's Mill he commanded the battalion that crossed the Warwick River, captured a line of rifle pits, and opened a gap in the enemy's line. In this engagement he was seriously wounded and his obituary published in Vermont. He survived, however, and was promoted to Major of the 3rd Vermont. Major Pingree was brother to Captain Stephen M. Pingree, 4th Vermont (see preceding narrative).

27. OR, 527-528, 623-624, 661; *Historical Sketch of the 15th Regiment New Jersey Volunteers* (Trenton: William S. Sharp Printer, 1880) 7; Clarke letter, 24 December 1862; Evander Law to Edward P. Alexander, 15 October 1866; *New York Times*, 21 December 1862; Supplement, 783-784. In addition to the 54th and 57th North Carolina, elements of the 4th Alabama (also of Law's brigade) and 16th North Carolina (Pender's brigade) participated in this attack. Lieutenant Martin reported that the rebels approached to within 400 yards of his battery (Supplement, 760).

28. Benedict, 344; "Vermont at Fredericksburg"; Evander Law to Edward P. Alexander, 15 October 1866; "Reminiscences of Emanuel Anther Peterson", Civil War Collection, State Archives of North Carolina; Barney diary, 13 December 1862 entry; Abbott letter, 15 December 1862; Dubois Memoir, 190; Buck letter, 15 December 1862; Clarke letter, 24 December 1862. According to Private Dubois, the 3rd Vermont, while hunkered behind the crest, was plainly visible to the Confederate skirmishers; if true, this information was not communicated to Law's North Carolinians who were genuinely surprised when Seaver's men delivered their sudden volley. As the 3rd Vermont charged onto the field it was accompanied by some of the Jerseymen previously driven from the railroad embankment. See Camille Baquet, *History of the First Brigade New Jersey Volunteers From 1861-1865* (Trenton: McCrellish and Quigley, 1910) 228.
29. "Vermont at Fredericksburg"; Evander Law to Edward P. Alexander, 15 October 1866; Supplement, 784; "From the 26th Regiment, Camp Near King George's Courthouse", *Newark Daily Mercury*, 27 December 1862. It is unclear what General Law hoped to accomplish by throwing two unsupported regiments of infantry against an entire division of the Sixth Corps, the latter supported by 5 batteries of well positioned Federal artillery.
30. Buck letter, 15 December 1862; Abbott letter, 15 December 1862; Dubois Memoir, 191.
31. Corporal Clarke states that the 3rd Vermont came onto the field from behind the crest formed in line of battle (Clarke letter, 24 December 1862). The Vermonters must have learned some useful lessons on the skirmish line at Fredericksburg. Seven months later, at Funkstown, Maryland, the brigade repulsed three Confederate lines of battle while deployed in a two mile long unsupported skirmish line (Benedict, 389-394).
32. OR, 533; Supplement, 793-794.
33. OR, 141; Benedict, 192, 345; Barney diary, 14 December 1862 entry; Murphy diary, 14 December 1862 entry; John Pitridge to John Capen, 10 January 1863, UVt; Robert Pratt to brother Sid, 15 December 1862, Bound Manuscripts–vol. 323, FSNMP; Lewis A. Grant letter, 4 January 1884; "Colonel Grant to Adjutant General Washburn, 17 December, 1862" in *Burlington (Daily) Free Press*, 26 December 1862;

The Pitridge quotes have been edited for spelling. The casualty figures cited for the 5th and 6th Vermont are totals, which do not distinguish between the fighting of 13 and 14 December. Private Pratt, however, gives the losses for 14 December as 1 killed and 20 wounded. Although the number of wounded given by Pratt does not match the official figure of 12 (OR, 141), it suggests that the bulk of the casualties in the 5th Vermont were from 14 December.

34. Murphy diary, 14 December, 1862 entry; Pitridge letter, 10 January 1863; Lester Hack to friend, 17 December 1862, excerpted in "… This Thing Will Never Be Settled …", James E. Peterson, editor, *Vermont History News,* March-April 1989, 40. The temperature at 2 p.m. was 63˚, at 9 p.m. it was 51˚ (Krick, 80).

35. OR, 530, 533; Supplement, 794; Barney diary, 15 December 1862 entry; Murphy diary, 15 December, 1862 entry; Stevens, 172; Sergeant William B. Stevens letter, 22 December 1862; Mellish letter, 18 December 1862. The temperature at 2 p.m. was 68.5˚, at 9 p.m. 60˚ (Krick, 80).

36. Murphy Diary, 16, 17, 18 December 1862 entries; Mellish letter, 18 December 1862 ["almost demolished"].

37. OR, 141; General Albion Howe to Major Charles Mundee, 19 December 1862, Letter Book 2nd Division, VI Army Corps, Records of Territorial Commands, RG 98, National Archives. The official losses in each regiment are as follows: 61 - 2nd, 11 – 3rd, 56 – 4th, 13 – 5th, 1 – 6th, 226 NJ. In his letter to Major Mundee, General Howe indicates that the losses in Companies D and G, 2nd Vermont, were especially heavy but gives no numbers.

38. OR, 141; "Vermont at Fredericksburg"; Stevens, 169-171; Jonathan Letterman M.D., *Medical Recollections of the Army of the Potomac* (New York: D. Appleton and Company, 1866) 52-63, 70-73; William Warren Potter M.D., *Reminiscences of Field Service with the Army of the Potomac* (Reprint from the Buffalo Medical and Surgical Journal, Oct. and Nov. 1889) 10-12.

39. OR, 532-533; Stephen M. Pingree to Cousin Augustus, 13 February 1863, VHS; Henry Whiting to Lieutenant E. Mattocks, 2 February 1863, Volunteer Service Records of Henry Whiting, RG 94; Chester K. Leach to wife, 5 February 1863, UVt. In his letter to Lieutenant Mattocks at Sixth Corps Headquarters, Whiting explained his resigna-

tion as follows: "Though the first Col. mustered into service of the first five Vermont Regiments, I am the only one holding that office now, and of the Field and Staff of the first three Regiments I am the only one remaining. Hence I have served an age and am entitled to an honorable discharge."

40. OR, 530; Pension Records of Charles H. Joyce and Nathan Lord, RG 94; Benedict—undated note; Francis E. Rew to mother, 27 December 1862, Bound Manuscripts—vol. 400, FSNMP ["bitter spirit … break him"]; Stephen M. Pingree to Cousin Augustus, 17 January 1863, VHS. Lieutenant Colonel Foster, of the 4th Vermont, remained with the regiment, as second in command, after the return of Colonel Charles B. Stoughton, who had been on sick leave during the Fredericksburg battle (Pension Record of Charles B. Stoughton, RG94).

41. William B. Stevens letter, 22 December 1862; "Colonel Grant to Adjutant General Washburn, 17 December, 1862" in *Burlington (Daily) Free Press*, 26 December 1862; Edward P. Stone to family, 23 December 1862, VHS; Murphy diary, 18 December 1862 entry; William F. Fox, *Regimental Losses in the American Civil War 1861-1865* (Albany: Brandow Printing Company, 1898) 116. Harrison's Landing is a point on the north bank of the James River to which the Army of the Potomac retreated after the Seven Days Battles, 25 June—1 July 1862. Toward the end of December the Vermont Brigade moved from its temporary camp at Belle Plain to a more permanent one near White Oak Church, Virginia where it spent the rest of the winter of 1862-1863.

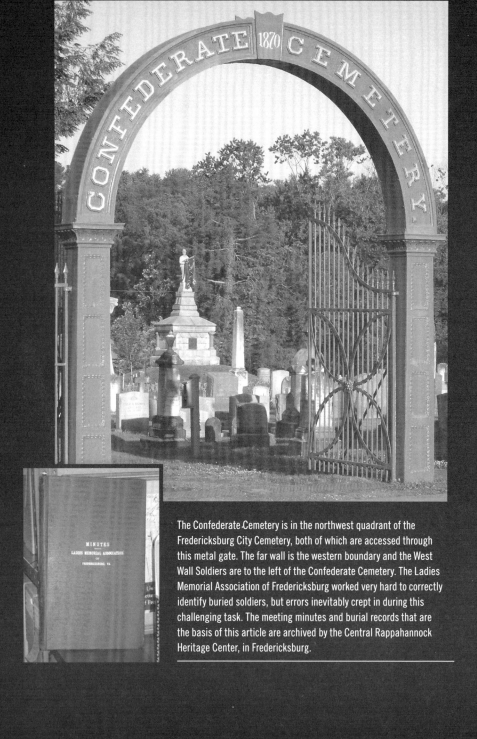

The Confederate Cemetery is in the northwest quadrant of the Fredericksburg City Cemetery, both of which are accessed through this metal gate. The far wall is the western boundary and the West Wall Soldiers are to the left of the Confederate Cemetery. The Ladies Memorial Association of Fredericksburg worked very hard to correctly identify buried soldiers, but errors inevitably crept in during this challenging task. The meeting minutes and burial records that are the basis of this article are archived by the Central Rappahannock Heritage Center, in Fredericksburg.

West Wall Soldiers

By Roy B. Perry Jr.

In May of 1866, just over a year after Appomattox, the Ladies Memorial Association of Fredericksburg established themselves and recorded the following statement of purpose in the minutes of a meeting held on June 1st, 1866:

> Our association proposes to preserve a record, and as far as possible, mark the spot where every Confederate soldier is buried in this vicinity, whether he fell on these memorable fields or otherwise died in the Service. To the bereaved throughout our suffering South, we pledge ourselves to spare no exertions to accomplish this work.
>
> In a land stripped of enclosures and forest, desolated and impoverished as ours, we cannot without aid guard these graves from exposure and possible desecration. We can only cover them with our native sod and with ___care, garland them with the wildflowers from the fields. But with the generous aid and cordial cooperation of those who have suffered less, but who feel as deeply as we do on this subject, we confidently hope to accomplish far more. To purchase and adorn a cemetery; to remove thither the sacred dust scattered all over this region and to erect some enduring tribute to the memory of our gallant dead.

The Ladies Memorial Association purchased land and established a Confederate Cemetery adjacent to the Fredericksburg Cemetery. They gathered the remains of Confederate dead from the nearby battlefields and brought them to a final resting place, recording their names as best they could. One by one, the Association recorded 3,553 Confederate dead, but there was a challenge in doing so since many soldiers had been buried for several years already and record keeping had sometimes been sketchy. Soldiers recovered in the field were often unknown. The best chance to correctly identify a man occurred when he died in a hospital, but even then there were no identity tags and some names were clearly misspelled by tired and busy attendants. Corrections have been made, as feasible.

The records maintained by the Association also give us the details of how the region handled the aftermath of the battles fought in and around Fredericksburg. Bodies were found "near Hazel Run," and on the "inside of Marye's enclosure back of the house." One note states that bodies were found on the "side Marye's Hill under the breastworks." Another note says others were found, "over the Hill on the edge of Haydon's cornfield." A group of remains were collected from "the flat between Howison's Mill and the dam near the Run." Bodies were brought to the attention of the Association as they were found. The records note bodies being "reported by Mrs. Anne Fitzhugh," or "by Mr. Lee Harrison.," and by others.

On November 1, 1888, several members of the Association gathered at the Fredericksburg Cemetery to record the names of the Confederate soldiers buried along its western perimeter wall. This area was where burials had occurred during the war and before the Confederate Cemetery had been established. The names of the soldiers were inscribed onto wooden post, which served as identification markers, but which also must have been fading. The Ladies Memorial Association recorded 174 names that day, but there were actually 179 burials where they were working. A note on page 86 of the roster states: "Some additional grave posts over private graves." In addition, though, it is possible that there were graves that had become unmarked by 1888. Along the rows of these Confederate dead are gaps between graves that could be remains where wooden posts were lost before the Ladies Memorial Association wrote out their roster.

There are already inventories of the graves in both cemeteries, done by Robert A. Hodge and Robert K. Krick. This list is meant to give details of the men buried along the City Cemetery's western boundary, noting the page in the original 1888 minute book where the soldiers are listed, including the sequential number that the Association used to identify each entry, and locating graves that were not visible when Robert Hodge developed his list. Also provided is the National Archives information for each soldier and a note on any variations in spelling. The documents used for this list are below:

In the Central Rappahannock Heritage Center, Fredericksburg VA:
Minutes of the Ladies Memorial Association of Fredericksburg, by the Ladies Memorial Association.
Roster of the Dead in the Confederate Cemetery at Fredericksburg, Virginia, by the Ladies Memorial Association.

In the Central Rappahannock Regional Library, Fredericksburg VA:
Tombstone Locations and Data in the Fredericksburg City Cemetery, compiled by Robert A. Hodge, 1988.
These We Know: Brief Biographical Sketches of 644 of the More Than 3500 Confederate Soldiers Buried in Fredericksburg, VA, compiled by Robert A. Hodge, 1993.
The Roster of Confederate Soldiers, 1861-1865, 14 volumes, Janet B. Hewett, ed., Broadfoot Publishing Co., Wilmington NC 1995-1996.

At the top of the Association's roster is the following note: "Names &c of Confederate soldiers buried near western wall in the 'Fredericksburg Cemetery' from information obtained directly from the grave posts on November 1st 1888." Another note is written across the last column of the first page, as follows: "All these names, ending with J. L. Burton on page 86, are recorded in due order in which they stand beginning at the North end of the row next to the Western Wall of the 'Fredericksburg Cemetery.' Nov. 1st 1888."

The chart on the following pages below shows the current location of the soldiers, as recorded by the author, comparing them to the record developed in 1888. The Ladies Memorial Association began at the north end of the row closest to the wall and moved south, toward William Street. They then turned around and followed the next three rows south to north. In the following list, each row is listed north to south, keeping the sequence of the LMA roster intact, but in reverse order for rows two, three, and four. The field examination showed that some of the markers had been moved from their original site or become broken and lost. With the permission of the Ladies Memorial Association of Fredericksburg, which is still an active organization, the Sons of Confederate Veterans, Matthew Fontaine Maury Camp 1722 replaced some of the missing stones.

The following list contains details on each of these men who came to be buried in the Fredericksburg City Cemetery during the Civil War.

Current position of West Wall graves (name on stone) starting at the north end of row nearest wall.		Position of graves indicated by 1888 LMA records.	
Stephen R. Marchman	ARK (new stone)	Steph. Marchman	ARK
Wm. C. Lynch	TENN	Wm. C. Lynch	TENN
Finly Collins	ARK	Finley Collins	ARK
Jno. M. Placer	ARK	Jno. M. Placer	ARK
Wm. R. Armstrong	ARK	Wm. R. Armstrong	ARK
Morgan Luster	ARK	Morgan Luster	ARK
Blank stone		Unknown	
Sam Tubbs	ARK	Sam Tubbs	ARK
Y.B. Brandy	ARK	Y.B. Brandy	ARK
J. Dabney LT.	VA	NOT LISTED	
Fred Myer	ARK	Fred Myer	ARK
William H. Roach	ARK	Wm. H. Roach	ARK
T.F. Henry	ARK	T.F. Henry	ARK
Horace Moore	ARK	Horace Moore	ARK
Wm. H. Johnson	ARK	Wm. H. Johnson	ARK
Jas. H. Heath	TENN	Jas. A. Heath	TENN
L.W. Wilder	ARK	L.W. Wilder	ARK
J.C. Handison	ARK	J.C. Handison	ARK
B. Cathon	TENN	B. Cathon	TENN
Wm. Daller	ARK	Wm. Daller	ARK
Saml. Robinson	TENN	Saml. Robinson	TENN
Nathan Young	ARK	Nathan Young	ARK
C.C. Overstreet	ARK	C.C. Overstreet	ARK
John Bullock	ARK	John Bullock	ARK
Jos. Rife	ARK	Jos. Rife	ARK
Jno. Farrs	ARK	John Farrs	ARK
S.L. Hicks	ARK	S.L. Hicks	ARK
Robt. McRoberts	ARK	Robt. McRoberts	ARK
D.A. Clengan	ARK	D.A. Clengan	ARK

W.P. Layman	ARK		W.P. Layman	ARK
Benj. Scott	ARK		Benj. Scott	ARK
Walter French	ARK		Walter French	ARK
Jos. Ball	ARK		Jos. Ball	ARK
Jas. M. Stedham	ARK		Jas. M. Stedham	ARK
Edwd. Letty	NC		Edwd. Letty	NC
J. Harrer	TENN		J. Harrer	TENN
T. Sager	NC (new stone)		T. Sarger	NC
Addison D. Stott	NC		Addison D. Stott	NC
Bradshaw	NC		John Bradshaw	NC
Levi Griffin	NC		Levi Griffin	NC
Pridgan	NC		"Pridgan"	NC
Harrell	TENN		"Harrell"	TENN
Mike O'Donnell	ARK		Mike O'Donnell	ARK
Wm. Colwell	TENN		Wm. Colwell	TENN
Jas. Taylor	NC		James Taylor	NC
J.B. Pope	VA (new stone)		J.B. Pope	Va
Reub. J. Edwards	ARK		Reubn J. Edwards	ARK
Richd. Corbit	NC		Richd Corbit	NC
Blank stone			Unknown	
Richd. C. Pitts	VA		Richd C. Pitts	Va
W.J. Sawyer	NC		W.J. Sawyer	NC
E. Dale	NC		E. Dale	NC
J.B. Henderson	NC		J.B. Henderson	NC
J. Mashman	NC		J. Mashman	NC
Norton Trots	NC		Norton Trots	NC
Mose	VA		"Mose"	Va
Pittman	NC		"Pittman"	NC
John C. Damson	ARK		John C. Damson	ARK
J.A. Pope	NC		J.A. Pope	NC
H.N. Lynch D2	GA		Henry N. Lynch	Ga
J.B. Clark	MISS			
Space				
Walter Carter	NC		Walter Carter	NC

Clem Paddy	NC	Clem Paddy NC	
Vaughn Carter	VA	Vaughn Carter	Va
W. Sutton	NC	W. Sutton	NC
Edmd. Tilly	NC	Edmd. Tilly NC	
J.W. Allen	VA	J.W. Allen	Va
A. Walker	GA	A. Walker	Ga
A.E. Cosser	NC	A.E. Cosser NC	
W. Gatewood	NC	W. Gatewood	NC
J.E. Bender	NC	J.F. Bender	NC
Dr. Millsops	ARK	Dr. Millsops ARK	
J.E. Cox	NC	J.E. Cox	NC
J.H. Budd	NC	J.H. Budd	NC
Robt. McCance	ARK	Robt. McCance	ARK
Hollaway	NC	"Hollaway" NC	
E.G. Christian	NC	E.G. Christian	NC
L. Davis	NC	L. Davis	NC
D. Parker	ARK	D. Parker	ARK
Wm. Lackey	NC	Wm. Lackey NC	
Blank stone		Unknown	
J.G. Williams	ARK	J.G. Williams	ARK
D. Grinnell	NC	D. Grinnell	NC
Jos. Hubbard	NC	Jos. Hubbard	NC
Lawrence Stamess	NC	Lawrence Stamess	NC
Jas. Jerrold	NC	Jas. Jerrold NC	
W.K. Leach	ARK	W.K. Leach AK	
Sam Stevens	ARK	Sam. Stevens	ARK
D. Duvall	ARK	D. Duvall	ARK
Blank stone		Unknown	
Blank stone		Unknown	
J.W.E. Allen	VA (new stone)		
W.T. Cummings	LA	W.T. Comming Capt	LA

First row ends here, next to William Street

Current position of West Wall graves (name on stone) starting at north end of second row from wall.		Position of graves indicated by 1888 LMA records.	
Sev. Moulbry	ARK	Sev. Moulbry	ARK
A. Brode	VA	A. Brode	Va
N.P. Oliver	NC	N.P. Oliver	NC
Sevear Marbang	ARK	Sevear Marbang	ARK
Geo. Williams	NC	Geo. Williams	NC
Geo. Fitzgerald	NC	Geo. Fitzgerald	NC
Blank stone			
Jos. Butting	NC	Jos. Butting	NC
Francis Lewis	NC	Francis Lewis	NC
R. Everett	NC	F. Liverman	NC
F. Liverman	NC	R. Everett	NC
J.L. Bland	NC	J.L. Bland	NC
Jos. Greer	NC	Jos. Greer	NC
Geo. W. Joice	NC	Geo. W. Joice	NC
Blank stone		Unknown	
Edward Greer	NC	Edward Greer	NC
Blank stone		Unknown	
A. Bondis	VA	A. Bondis	Va
Noah Clark	NC	Noah Clarke	NC
Jos. T.J. Wroten	MISS	Jos. T.J. Wroten	MISS
J.A.J. Trusell	MISS	J.A.J. Trusell	MISS
Space		Unknown	
T.J. Owens	MISS	J.T. Owens	MISS
W.S. Brandon	MISS	W.S. Brandon	MISS
Blank stone	Unknown		
W.L. Cage	MISS	W.L. Cage	MISS
Alex Snead	MISS	Alex. Snead	MISS
Cosley Gardner	NC	Cosley Gardner	NC
Stone very worn		J.B. Clark	MISS

Current position of West Wall graves, continued.

J.A. Bohannon	NC	J.A. Bohannon	NC
Baughan	NC	"Baughan"	NC
J. Mashman	NC		
Blank stone			
Jno. Witherspoon	MISS		
C.S. Samuel	GA	G.S. Samuel	Ga
Blank stone			
Blank stone			
Blank stone	Unknown		
Blank stone	Unknown		
Blank stone	Unknown		
Blank stone	Unknown		
Blank stone	Unknown		
Blank stone	Unknown		
Blank stone	Unknown		
Blank stone	Unknown		
E.E. Stephen	MISS	E.E. Stephens	MISS
John Gatewood	NC	Unknown	
Space	Jas. –		
Blank stone	Unknown		
Newton Higgen	GA	Newton Higgen	Ga
Blank stone	Unknown		
Blank stone	Unknown		
Space		A.W. White	MISS
W.G. Willig Segt	LA	W.G. Willig, Sergt.	La
Second row ends here			

Fredericksburg History & Biography

Current position of West Wall graves (name on stone) starting at north end of third row from wall.		Position of graves indicated by 1888 LMA records.	
James Southard (new stone)		James Southard	
John A. Oliver	TEX	John A. Oliver	TEX
Jas. A. Foster	MISS	Jas. A Foster	MISS
M.M. Herbert	MISS	M.M. Herbert	MISS
R.M. Day	MISS	R.M. Day	MISS
Blank stone	Unknown		
J.C. Clark	VA	J.C. Clarke	MISS
R.M. Perry	VA	R.M. Perry	MISS
S.L. Harden	MISS (new stone)	S.L. Harden	MISS
Jos. A. Allen (small, non-military stone) also appears to read 17th Mississippi Regt, killed at Fredericksburg on 3 May 1863		E.P. Miller, Lt.	MISS
David McCrey	VA	David McCrey	MISS
J.A. Daly	VA	J.A. Daly	MISS
Gordon Shepherd	VA	Gordon Shephard	MISS
B.C. Blackstone	MISS	B.C. Blackstone	MISS
N. Born	NC	S.S. Wicks	MISS
S.H. Beamm	MISS	S.H. Beamm	MISS
Eldridge	TENN	"Eldridge"	TENN
S.S. Wicks	MISS	N. Born	NC
J.D. Woodard	MISS	J.D. Woodward	MISS
D.L. Evans K 24	GA	D.L. Evans	Ga
Lacy Stewart K 24	GA	Lacy Stewart, Lt.	Ga
Third row ends here			

Current position of West Wall graves (name on stone) starting at north end of fourth row from wall.		Position of graves indicated by 1888 LMA records.	
J.L. Burton	NC	J.L. Burton	NC
Blank stone		Unknown	
McKee	MISS	J.M. Old	MISS
J.M. Old	MISS	"McKee"	MISS
J.S. Rogers	MISS	Unknown	
Blank stone		J.S. Rogers	MISS
T.F. Coleman	MISS	T.F. Coleman	MISS
Blank stone	Unknown		
Blank stone	Unknown		
Space		R.B. Adams	MISS
Blank stone	Unknown		
Space		Jos. A. Miller	MISS
J.H. Smith Sergt	MISS	J.H. Smith, Sergt	MISS
J.W. Shackelford	MISS	J.W. Shackleford	MISS
Fourth row ends here			

Adams, Robert B. (stone missing)
Private, Companies E and D, 13th Regiment Mississippi Infantry
Born in South Carolina, Adams was a 19 or 20 year old farmer, 5 feet 7 inches tall, with dark complexion, dark hair, and gray eyes when he enlisted at Decatur, Mississippi, on 23 March 1861. He traveled 218 miles to the point of rendezvous at Corinth, Mississippi, arriving there by 17 May 1861. During September-October 1861 he was sick at Warrenton, Virginia. Appointed Corporal on 27 April 1862, he soon after became ill again and was in General Hospital #18 (Gleaners) in Richmond, Virginia from 26 May until 2 June 1862. He was killed in the second battle of Fredericksburg on 3 May 1863.
References: *LMA minutes (1888), pages 11 (#182) and 86. Roster of Confederate Soldiers 1861-1865, Vol. I, page 50. Hodge, "These We Know", page 7. National Archives Catalog ID: 586957, Roll 0210, page 12, Publication number M269.*

The Confederates buried in the Fredericksburg Cemetery were concentrated along its western boundary wall, but are still mixed in with many others, which becomes evident when flags are placed on Memorial Day.

Allen, J. William (stone reads: J.W. Allen VA)
Private, Company D, 2nd Regiment North Carolina Infantry (State Troops)
William Allen enlisted at Goldsboro, North Carolina on 29 May 1861 and died on 8 September 1861 of acute diarrhea. William H. Norton was paid for the burial of this soldier, at No. 2 Hospital, Fredericksburg, Virginia, on 8 September 1861, in the amount of $15.
References: *LMA minutes (1888), pages 3 (#27) and 83. Noted as Allen, William A. in the Roster of Confederate Soldiers 1861-1865, Vol. I, page 126. National Archives Catalog ID: 586957, Roll 0106, page 3, Publication number M270.*

Allen, John W. E. (new stone reads: J.W.E. Allen VA)
Corporal, Company K, 30th Virginia Infantry
John Allen enlisted on 19 August 1861 and died on 5 October 1861 in a hospital at Fredericksburg.
References: *LMA minutes (1888), pages 3 (#2) and 83. Noted as Allen, John W. in the Roster of the Confederate Soldiers 1861-1865, Vol. I, page 117.*

Hodge, "These We Know," page 8. National Archives Catalog ID: 586957, Roll 0760, page 3, Publication number M 324.

The Matthew Fontaine Maury Camp 1722 of the Sons of Confederate Veterans placed a new marker on 29 March 2008.

Armstrong, William K. (stone reads: Wm. R. Armstrong ARK)
Private, Company C, 1st Arkansas Infantry
On 8 May 1861, William Armstrong, born in Mississippi and a clerk by occupation, enlisted at Camden, Arkansas at the age of 20. On 19 May 1861, he mustered into Confederate service at Lynchburg, Virginia. Armstrong was 5 feet 11 inches tall, with olive eyes, and sandy hair. His complexion was fair. He died of measles at Camp Jackson, near Fredericksburg, on 25 June 1861.
References: *Listed as Armstrong, William R. in the LMA minutes (1888), pages 7 (#90) and 81. Noted as Armstrong, William K. in the Roster of Confederate Soldiers 1861-1865, Vol. I, page 216. Hodge, "These We Know," page 11. National Archives Catalog ID: 586957, Roll 0046, page 3, Publication number M317.*

Bandy, William A. (stone reads: Y.B. Brandy ARK)
Private, Company E, 1st Regiment Arkansas Infantry
On 26 April 1861, William Bandy, a school teacher, enlisted at Benton Arkansas. He was 36 years old. He mustered into Confederate service on 19 May 1861 at Lynchburg, Virginia and died of disease in Fredericksburg, on 20 June 1861.
References: *LMA minutes (1888), pages 7 (#86) and 81. Noted as Bandy, William A. in the Roster of Confederate Soldiers 1861-1865, Vol. I, page 349. National Archives Catalog ID: 586957, Roll 0046, page 3, Publication number M317.*

A new stone marker was placed at Bandy's grave site on 29 March 2008 by the Matthew Fontaine Maury Camp 1722.

Baugh, John, F. (stone reads: Baughan NC)
Private, Company C, 33rd Regiment North Carolina Infantry (State Troops)
On 1 March 1862, at the age of 23, John Baugh a resident of Cabarrus County, North Carolina, volunteered to serve in the Confederate Army and was sworn into service by W. A. Patterson at Concord, North Carolina. His

service records show that he died of disease in Fredericksburg on 8 April 1862.
References: *Listed as Baughn in the LMA minutes (1888), page 84, but not included on the list of soldiers listed that year. Noted as Baugh, John F. in the Roster of Confederate Soldiers 1861-1865, Vol. I, page 449. National Archives Catalog ID: 586957, Roll 0377, page 17, Publication number M270.*

Bawl, Joseph J. (stone reads: Jos. Ball ARK)
Private, Company F, 1st Regiment Arkansas Infantry
Bawl was a farmer by trade. At the age of 25, he enlisted for one year. He mustered into Confederate service on 19 May 1861 in Lynchburg, Virginia. His service record shows that he was present on 30 June 1861, with no other reference given. The LMA minutes indicate that he died of disease in or near Fredericksburg.
References: *LMA minutes (1888), pages 5 (#62) and 82. Listed as Bawl, Joseph J. in the Roster of Confederate Soldiers 1861-1865, Vol. I, page 453. National Archives Catalog ID: 586957, Roll 0046, page 3, Publication number M317.*

Bender, Frank J. (stone reads: J.E. Bender NC)
Private, Company G, 2nd Regiment North Carolina Infantry (State Troops)
This 22 year old resident of Jones County, North Carolina enlisted at Trenton, North Carolina on 24 May 1861, to serve for the duration of the war. He died in Hospital #2 at Fredericksburg, Virginia on 12 September 1861. His Captain took possessions of his effects, which amounted to $17.25. William H. Norton was paid $15 to bury him.
References: *LMA minutes (1888), pages 3 (#23) and 83. Roster of Confederate Soldiers 1861-1865, Vol. II, page 20. North Carolina Roster, Vol. 3, page 442. Hodge, "These We Know," page 16. National Archives Catalog ID: 586957, Roll 0106, page 3, Publication number M270.*

Blackstone, B. C. (stone reads: B.C. Blackstone MISS)
Private, Company C, 18th Regiment Mississippi Volunteers
This 52 year old man enlisted on 18 January 1863 at Fredericksburg, Virginia, to serve for 2 years. He was killed at or near Fredericksburg on 3 May 1863.
References: *LMA minutes (1888), pages 9 (#142) and 85. Roster of Confederate Soldiers 1861-1865, Vol. II, page 118. Hodge, "These We*

Know," page 17. National Archives Catalog ID: 586957, Roll 0263, page 4, Publication number M269.

Bland, John L. (stone reads: J.L. Bland NC)
Corporal, Company I, 2nd Regiment North Carolina Infantry (State Troops)
This resident of Craven County, North Carolina enlisted on 29 May 1861 at New Berne, North Carolina, to serve for the duration of the war. He was 18 years old. He mustered into Confederate service as a Corporal and died at Camp Potomac, Virginia on 23 October 1861.
References: *LMA minutes (1888), pages 11 (#162) and 85. Roster of Confederate Soldiers 1861-1865, Vol. II, page 136. National Archives Catalog ID: 586957, Roll 0106, page 3, Publication number M 270.*

Blann, Stephen H. (stone reads: S.H. Beamm MISS)
Private, Company E, 13th Regiment Mississippi Volunteers
Stephen Blann was born in Sumter County, Alabama, and enlisted on 14 May 1861 at Corinth, Mississippi, for one year. He re-enlisted on 1 February 1862. In April or May of that year he drowned in the Rappahannock River at Fredericksburg. He was reported as being "a good soldier."
References: *LMA minutes (1888), pages 9 (#144) and 85. Roster of Confederate Soldiers 1861-1865, Vol. II, page 142. Hodge, "These We Know," page 18. National Archives Catalog ID: 586957, Roll 0211, page 11, Publication number M269.*

Bode, August (stone reads: A. Brode VA)
Private, Company A, 30th Regiment Virginia Infantry
Brode is listed in the LMA register as a Private in Company A, 30th Regiment Virginia Infantry, but his name does not appear in the unit roster. A likely match for this soldier is August Bode, who enlisted on 22 April 1861 for one year. His service records show that he was detached in Goldsboro as a baker. Bode was also listed sick at home in Fredericksburg Virginia, but with no date stated.
References: *Listed as A. Brode in the LMA minutes (1888), pages 11 (#168) and 85. Listed as Bode, August in the Roster of Confederate Soldiers 1861-1865, Vol. II, page 168. National Archives Catalog ID: 586957, Roll 0761, page 10, Publication number M324.*

Bohannan, John A. (stone reads: J.A. Bohannon NC)
Private, Company H, 22nd North Carolina Infantry
On 1 June 1861, John Bohanan enlisted at Stokes County, North Carolina, to serve for one year. He was 21 years old and paid bounty of $10. He was reported sick on 25 August 1861 at Fredericksburg, Virginia and died of disease there on 19 September 1861.
References: *Listed as J.A. Bohannan in the LMA minutes (1888), pages 11 (#166) and 84. Listed as Bohanan, John A. in the Roster of Confederate Soldiers 1861-1865, Vol. II, page 174. Hodge, "These We Know," page 19. National Archives Catalog ID: 2133276, Roll 0031, page 3, Publication number M 347.*

Boon, Nathan S. (stone reads: N. Born NC)
Private, Company A, 5th Regiment North Carolina Infantry (State Troops)
A 33-year old resident of Chatham County, North Carolina, Nathan Boon enlisted in Wake County on 15 July 1862, to serve for the duration of the war. He was wounded in the head at Gettysburg, on 1 July 1863, but rejoined the company in November-December 1863. He was again wounded, in the left thigh, and captured near Wilderness Tavern, Virginia on 9 May 1864. On 23 May 1864, he was listed as being in a hospital in Fredericksburg. There is no record of his death, except for his body buried in the Fredericksburg City Cemetery.
References: *Listed as N. Boon in the LMA minutes (1888), pages 9 (#146) and 85. Listed as Boon, Nathan S. in the Roster of Confederate Soldiers 1861-1865, Vol. II, page 202. North Carolina Roster, Vol. 4, page 132. Hodge, "These We Know," pages 19-20. National Archives Catalog ID: 586957, Roll 0146, page 12, Publication number M270.*

Bradshaw, John (stone reads: Bradshaw NC)
Corporal, Company G, 33rd Regiment North Carolina Infantry (State Troops)
John Bradshaw was 28 years old and a farmer from Cumberland County, North Carolina, when he enlisted as a Corporal on 2 September 1861. He mustered into Confederate service the same day. Bradshaw was listed as a prisoner of war on 9 August 1862 at Cedar Run, Virginia and was part of a prisoner exchange on 1 September 1862. Upon his return to duty on 15 November 1862, he was reduced in rank to Private. Private Bradshaw was killed at Chancellorsville on 1 May 1863.

References: LMA minutes (1888), pages 5 (#56) and 82. Roster of Confederate Soldiers 1861-1865, Vol. I, page 294. National Archives Catalog ID: 586957, Roll 0378, page 3, Publication number M270.

    A stone marker was placed at Bradshaw's grave site on 29 March 2008 by the Matthew Fontaine Maury Camp 1722

Brandon, William S. (stone reads: W.S. Brandon MISS)
Private, Company D, 21st Regiment Mississippi Volunteers
Brandon was a single 30 year old overseer living at Woodville, Mississippi when he enlisted on 23 February 1862, at New Orleans, to serve for the duration of the war. He died at Fredericksburg, Virginia.
References: LMA minutes (1888), pages 11 (#157) and 84. Roster of Confederate Soldiers 1861-1865, Vol. II, page 311. Hodge, "These We Know," page 21. National Archives Catalog ID: 586957, Roll 0294, page 2, Publication number M 269.

Broaddus A. Thomas (stone reads: A. Bondis VA)
Corporal, Company H, 30th Regiment Virginia Infantry
The LMA register lists Bondis, A. as a Private in the 30th Virginia Infantry, but the unit roster shows no one by that name. A likely candidate for this soldier is Broaddus, Thomas A., who served as a Corporal in Company H of that unit.

    Thomas Broaddus was a 20 year farmer from Caroline County, Virginia, who enlisted on 1 April 1861 at Sparta, Virginia, to serve for one year. He was 5 feet 9 inches tall, fair complexion, with dark eyes and black hair. In November 1862 he was listed as sick at home and discharged on 22 December 1862 in a Camp near Fredericksburg.
References: LMA minutes (1888), pages 11 (#171) and 84. Roster of Confederate Soldiers 1861-1865, Vol. II, page 378. National Archives Catalog ID: 586957, Roll 0761, page 11, Publication number M 324.

Budd, Joseph H. (stone reads: J.H. Budd NC)
Private, Company I, 2nd Regiment North Carolina Infantry (State Troops)
A 23 year old Joseph Budd, in Craven County, North Carolina, enlisted on 31 May 1861, to serve for the duration of the war. He died in a hospital at Fredericksburg, on 14 September 1861.
References: LMA minutes (1888), pages 3 (#20) and 83. Roster of Confederate

Soldiers 1861-1865, Vol. II, page 516. North Carolina Roster, Vol. 3, page 463. Hodge, "These We Know," page 24. National Archives Catalog ID: 586957, Roll 0107, page 3, Publication number M270.

Bull, Frederick (name on stone: John Bull)
Private, Company C, 30th Regiment Virginia Infantry
Bull is not listed in the 1888 Minutes, nor is there record of any soldier by this name serving in any Virginia unit. The likely match for this soldier is Frederick Bull, who enlisted on 23 May 1861 at Fredericksburg, Virginia. Bull, who may well have been called John, died of typhoid pneumonia on 23 January 1862 in Fredericksburg.
References: *Bull, Frederick is in the Roster of Confederate Soldiers 1861-1865, Vol. III, page 8. National Archives Catalog ID: 586957, Roll 0761, page 5, Publication number M 324.*

Bullock, John A. (stone reads: John Bullock ARK)
Private, Company I, 1st Regiment Arkansas Infantry
John Bullock was a 17 year old clerk when he enlisted on 8 May 1861 at Monticello, Arkansas, to serve for one year. He was mustered into Confederate service at Lynchburg, Virginia on 19 May 1861. His service record contains no reference to his death.
References: *LMA minutes (1888), pages 7 (#72) and 81. Roster of Confederate Soldiers 1861-1865, Vol. III, page 13. Hodge, "These We Know," page 25. National Archives Catalog ID: 586957, Roll 0046, page 3, Publication number M317.*

Burton, John L. (stone reads: J.L. Burton NC)
Corporal, Company F, 4th Regiment North Carolina Infantry (State Troops)
Burton was a 19 year old resident of Wilson County, North Carolina when he enlisted at New Berne on 28 June 1861, to serve for the duration of the war. He became a prisoner of war, presumably during the Antietam campaign, and was paroled on 27 September 1862. He was also captured at Fredericksburg, Virginia, on 3 May 1863 and confined at the Old Capitol Prison in Washington D.C. until transferred to City Point, Virginia on 10 May 1863 for exchange. Following his promotion to Corporal he was wounded in the left leg and again captured, this time at Wilderness Tavern, Virginia on 15 May 1864. He died of his wounds on 16 June 1864.

References: *LMA minutes (1888), pages 11 (#190) and 86. Roster of Confederate Soldiers 1861-1865, Vol. III, page 76. North Carolina Roster, Vol. 4, page 69. Hodge, "These We Know," page 26. National Archives Catalog ID: 586957, Roll 0137, page 18, Publication number M 270.*

Buttery, Jordan L. (stone reads: Jos. Butting NC)
Private, Company G, 1st Regiment North Carolina Infantry (State Troops)
The LMA records list a Joseph Butting from the 1st North Carolina Infantry, but a search of the unit roster reveals Jordan Buttery as the most likely man. Buttery enlisted in June of 1861 at Plymouth, North Carolina, to serve for the duration of the war. He was 25 years old. He died in Fredericksburg on 10 December 1861.

References: *LMA minutes (1888), pages 9 (#126) and 85. Roster of Confederate Soldiers 1861-1865, Vol. III, page 101. Hodge, "These We Know," page 26. National Archives Catalog ID: 586957, Roll 0091, page 3, Publication number M 270.*

Cage, William L. (stone reads: W.L. Cage MISS)
2nd Lieutenant, Company D, 21st Regiment Mississippi Infantry
On 22 May 1861, William Cage enlisted, at the age of 40, at Woodville, Wilkinson County, Mississippi, to serve for the duration of the war. On 31 August 1861 he was listed as assigned to "Special duty as chief of Police Camp Dickens, Manassas." He was promoted to 1st Lieutenant on 1 July 1862. He was sick on furlough throughout November and December of 1862. William Cage died in Fredericksburg in April 1863.

References: *LMA minutes (1888), pages 9 (#110) and 84. Roster of Confederate Soldiers 1861-1865, Vol. III, page 122. National Archives Catalog ID: 586957, Roll 0294, page 12, Publication number M 269.*

Calwell, William C. (stone reads: Wm. Colwell TENN)
Private, Company D, 2nd Regiment Tennessee Infantry
On 1 May 1861, a 22-year old William Calwell enlisted in Bedford County, Tennessee, for one year. He mustered into Confederate service at Lynchburg, Virginia on 17 May 1861. Caldwell died 10 August 1861 at Fredericksburg.

References: *LMA minutes (1888), pages 5 (#50) and 82. Listed as Caldwell, William in the Roster of Confederate Soldiers 1861-1865, Vol. III, page 151.*

National Archives Catalog ID: 586957, Roll 0114, page 3, Publication number M268.

Carter, William (stone reads: Walter Carter NC)
Private, Company B, 2nd Regiment North Carolina Infantry (State Troops)
The 2nd North Carolina roster has no Walter Carter listed, but there is a William Carter. On 27 May 1861, at 21 years of age, William Carter enlisted at Wilson, North Carolina, to serve for the duration of the war. He died at Fredericksburg. On 3 September 1861, William H. Norton was paid $15 to bury him in the Fredericksburg City Cemetery. His effects were delivered to his father, who is not named.
References: *LMA minutes (1888), pages 3 (#32) and 82. Roster of Confederate Soldiers 1861-1865, Vol. III, page 269. Hodge, "These We Know," page 30. National Archives Catalog ID: 586957, Roll 0107, page 5, Publication number M270.*

Causey, Alfred E. (stone reads: A.E. Cosser NC)
Private, Company I, 22nd Regiment North Carolina Infantry (formerly 12th North Carolina Infantry, Volunteers)
Alfred Causey was a resident of Randolph County, North Carolina, when he enlisted there on 5 June 1861 and was mustered into Confederate service the same day. He was a farmer by trade and 51 years old. He died of unknown causes on 10 September 1861 at Fredericksburg, leaving a wife and four children behind.
References: *Listed as A.E. Cosser in the LMA minutes (1888), pages 3 (#25) and 83. Listed as Causey, Alfred E. in the Roster of Confederate Soldiers 1861-1865, Vol. III, page 308. National Archives Catalog ID: 586957, Roll 0286, pages 3 and 6, Publication number M270.*

Christian, N. H. (stone reads: E.G. Christian NC)
Private, Companies F and D, 12th Regiment North Carolina Infantry
There is no one listed in the 12th North Carolina roster with the initials E. G. The most likely match for this soldier is Christian, N. H., who enlisted at the age of 18 in Richmond, Virginia, date not stated. He worked in food preparation by trade. There is no record of him dying in Fredericksburg, but he fits the information provided in the 1888 Minutes.
References: *Listed as E.G. Christian in the LMA minutes (1888), pages 3*

(#17) and 83. Listed as Christian, N. H. in the Roster of Confederate Soldiers 1861-1865, Vol. III, page 393. National Archives Catalog ID: 586957, Roll 0202, page 2, Publication number M270.

Clark, J. C. (stone reads: J.C. Clark VA)
Private, Companies I and E, 13th Mississippi Infantry
On 29 October 1861, Clark enlisted at Montgomery, Alabama, for the duration of the war. On 8 November 1862, he was listed as sick in Culpeper, Virginia. In January of 1863 he was listed as ill in Ward 4 at the General Hospital, Farmville, Virginia, with catarrhal fever. He returned to duty on 12 January 1863, but on 9 February 1863 Clark was listed among those who died of disease in Fredericksburg.
References: *Listed as J.C. Clarke in the LMA minutes (1888), page 11 (#176) and 85. Listed as Clark J.C. In the Roster of Confederate Soldiers 1861-1865, Vol. III, page 417. National Archives Catalog ID: 586957, Roll 0212, page 7, Publication number M269.*

The West Wall Soldiers. View is toward the south.

Clarke, Noah (stone reads: Noah Clark NC)
Private, Companies E and D, 13th Regiment Mississippi Volunteers
On 15 May 1861, Noah Clarke, born in Alabaman, enlisted at Corinth City, Mississippi for one year. He was 23 years old and a farmer. He mustered into Confederate service on 17 May 1861 and died of disease on 20 March 1863 in Fredericksburg.
References: *LMA minutes (1888), pages 11 (#175) and 84. Roster of Confederate Soldiers 1861-1865, Vol. III, page 433. National Archives Catalog ID: 586957, Roll 0212, page 13, 15 Publication number M 269.*

Clarke, Thomas B. (stone reads: J.B. Clark MISS)
Private, Company H, 48th Regiment Mississippi Volunteers
Thomas Clarke enlisted at Vicksburg, Mississippi on 23 April 1862. He mustered into Confederate service for three years. On 10 August 1862, he was listed as sick at the General Hospital, Camp Winder, in Richmond, Virginia, but returned to duty on August 14th. He appears on a 9 May 1863 casualty report for Posey's Brigade and his service record shows that he was killed on 3 May 1862, at Chancellorsville.
References: *Listed as J.B. Clark in the LMA minutes (1888), pages 11 (#154) and 84. Listed as Clarke, Thomas B. in the Roster of Confederate Soldiers 1861-1865, Vol. III, page 434. National Archives Catalog ID: 586957, Roll 0416, pages 8-9, Publication number M 269.*

Clingan Davis Alexander (stone reads: D.A. Clengan ARK)
Private, Company B, 1st Regiment Arkansas Infantry
This soldier enlisted on 8 May 1861 at Little Rock, Arkansas. He died of measles on 25 July 1861 at Fredericksburg.
References: *Listed as D.A. Clengan in the LMA minutes (1888), page 5 (#66) and 82. Listed as Clingan, Davis A. in the Roster of Confederate Soldiers 1861-1865, Vol. III, page 465. National Archives Catalog ID: 586957, Roll 0046, page 2, Publication number M317.*

Coleman, T. F. (stone reads: T.F. Coleman MISS)
Private, Companies B and A, 13th Regiment Mississippi Infantry
Born in Winston County, Mississippi, this single farmer stood 6 foot 2 inches, had a fair complexion, light hair and blue eyes, and lived near Buckhorn, Mississippi. He traveled 142 miles to enlist at Corinth,

Mississippi. He mustered into Confederate service at Louisville, Mississippi on 5 March 1861, to serve for one year. He later re-enlisted for two more years. He was present at First Manassas, Leesburg, Garnett's Farm, Savage Station, Malvern Hill, Maryland Heights, and Sharpsburg. He was killed at Fredericksburg on 11 December 1862.

References: *LMA minutes (1888), pages 11 (#184) and 86. Roster of Confederate Soldiers 1861-1865, Vol. IV, page 25. Hodge, "These We Know," page 35. National Archives Catalog ID: 586957, Roll 0212, page 13, Publication number M269.*

Some time after the war, someone returned to place a foot marker in memory of this young man who had died at the age of 17. It is the only foot marker among the West Wall Soldiers.

Collins, Finley, (stone reads: Finly Collins ARK)

Private, Company G, 1ˢᵗ Regiment Arkansas Infantry

Finley Collins was 25 years old when he enlisted at Jacksonport, Arkansas on 5 May 1861 and mustered into Confederate service on 9 May 1861 at Lynchburg, Virginia. He died in a hospital at Fredericksburg, in June 1861.

References: *Listed as Finley Collins in the LMA minutes (1888), pages 7 (#92) and 81. Roster of Confederate Soldiers 1861-1865, Vol. IV, page 38. Hodge, "These We Knew, " pages 35-36. National Archives Catalog ID: 586957, Roll 0047, page 3, Publication number M317.*

Corbett, Richard (stone reads: Richd Corbit NC)

Private, Company D, 2ⁿᵈ Regiment North Carolina Infantry (State Troops)

On 31 May 1861, Richard Corbett, an 18 year old farmer of Wayne County, who had been born in Johnston County, North Carolina, enlisted for the duration of the war. He died in a hospital at Fredericksburg, on 15 August 1861.

References: *Listed as Richd Corbit in the LMA minutes (1888), pages 5 (#46) and 82. Listed as Corbett, Richard in the Roster of Confederate Soldiers 1861-1865, Vol. IV, page 134. North Carolina Roster, Vol. 3, page 414. Hodge, "These We Know," page 36. National Archives Catalog ID: 586957, Roll 0107, page 2, Publication number M270.*

Cothran, Benjamin F. (stone reads: B. Cathon TENN)
Corporal, Company B, 1st Regiment Tennessee Infantry
Cothran was 28 years old when he enlisted at Tullahoma, Tennessee on 29 April 1861, to serve for one year. He reenlisted on 27 April 1862 at Yorktown, Virginia, to serve for two more years and be promoted to Corporal. He was injured at Fredericksburg, on 13 December 1862. He is buried in the south section of the Fredericksburg City Cemetery, but a service record entry on 2 March 1863 lists him as a deserter.
References: *Listed as B. Cothan in the LMA minutes (1888), pages 7 (#77) and 81. Listed as Cothran, Benjamin F. in the Roster of Confederate Soldiers 1861-1865, Vol. IV, page 154. Hodge, "These We Know," page 37. National Archives Catalog ID: 586957, Roll 0107, pages 9 and 11, Publication number M268.*

Cox, James E. (stone reads: J.E. Cox NC)
Private, Company G, 2nd Regiment North Carolina Infantry (State Troops)
Cox was an 18 year old resident of Jones County, North Carolina when he enlisted on 24 May 1861, to serve for the duration of the war. He died in a hospital at Fredericksburg, on 15 September 1861.
References: *LMA minutes (1888), pages 3 (#21) and 83. Roster of Confederate Soldiers 1861-1865, Vol. IV, page 186. North Carolina Roster, Vol. 3, page 443. Hodge, "These We Know," page 38. National Archives Catalog ID: 586957, Roll 0107, page 7, Publication number M270.*

Cummings, W. T. (stone reads: W.T. Cummings LA)
Captain, Company B, 9th Regiment Louisiana Volunteers
Cummings joined on 7 July 1861, at Camp Moore, Louisiana. He was wounded at Second Manassas on 28 August 1862 and was on furlough from 18 November 1862 through February 1863, suffering from wounds. He was killed on 4 May 1863 at Fredericksburg, during the Chancellorsville campaign.
References: *Listed as W.T. Comming in the LMA minutes (1888), pages 7 (#96) and 83. Listed as Cummings, W.T. in the Roster of Confederate Soldiers 1861-1865, Vol. IV, page 299. Louisiana Roster, Vol. I-II, page 501. Hodge, "These We Know," page 40. National Archives Catalog ID: 586957, Roll 0204, page 13, Publication number M 320.*

Dabney, John W. (stone reads: J. Dabney LT. ARK)
Lieutenant, Company G, 30th Regiment Virginia Infantry
Born in 1828, Dabney was a clerk by occupation when he enlisted on 23 May 1861 with the rank of Sergeant. He was elected Lieutenant on 18 November 1861, but died of pneumonia on 20 January 1862 in Fredericksburg, Virginia.
References: *Lieutenant Dabney is not listed in the 1888 LMA minutes, which may mean that his marker was placed by family members. Roster of Confederate Soldiers 1861-1865, Vol. IV, page 330. Hodge, "These We Know," page 40. National Archives Catalog ID: 586957, Roll 0762, page 10, Publication number M324.*

Dale, Evans (stone reads: E. Dale NC)
Private, Company H, 2nd Regiment North Carolina Infantry (State Troops)
Evans Dale was a 19 year old farmer, born and residing in Duplin County, North Carolina, who enlisted in Wayne County on 27 May 1861, to serve for the duration of the war. He died in a hospital in Fredericksburg, on 26 August 1861.
References: *LMA minutes (1888), pages 5 (#42) and 82. Roster of Confederate Soldiers 1861-1865, Vol. IV, page 336. Hodge, "These We Know," page 41. North Carolina Roster, Vol. 3, page 453. National Archives Catalog ID: 586957, Roll 0108, page 3, Publication number M270.*

Daily, James A. (stone reads: J.A. Daly VA)
Private, Companies C and B, 13th Regiment Mississippi Volunteers
James Daily was born in Memphis, Tennessee. He enlisted at Brookhaven, Mississippi, on 4 August 1862. He was a bookkeeper by trade and 25 years of age. Daly died of disease on 7 April 1863 in Fredericksburg, Virginia.
References: *Although his stone reads that he was from Virginia, the LMA minutes (1888), pages 11 (#179) and 85, make clear he was from Mississippi. Listed as Daily, James A. in the Roster of Confederate Soldiers 1861-1865, Vol. IV, page 334. National Archives Catalog ID: 586957, Roll 0213, page 7, Publication number M269.*

Davis, Lauchlin (stone reads: L. Davis NC)
Private, Company C, 3rd Regiment North Carolina Infantry (State Troops)
Lauchlin Davis was a resident of Cumberland County and 20 years old

when he enlisted. He was mustered into Confederate service on 13 June 1861 at Fayetteville, North Carolina, for the duration of the war. He died on 15 September 1861, in a hospital at Fredericksburg. The cause of death is unknown.
References: *LMA minutes (1888), pages 3 (#16) and 83. Roster of Confederate Soldiers 1861-1865, Vol. IV, page 420. National Archives Catalog ID: 586957, Roll 0125, page 5, Publication number M270.*

Dawson, John C. (stone reads: John C. Damson ARK)
Private, Company B, 1st Regiment Arkansas Infantry
John Dawson was born in Alabama, in 1838. On 8 May 1861, he was a 23-year old clerk who lived in Clark County Arkansas when he enlisted at Little Rock, Arkansas. There is no further record of this man after 30 June 1861, but the Couch Genealogy of Arkansas Soldiers shows that several men from this regiment died from measles in Fredericksburg.
References: *LMA minutes (1888), pages 3 (#35) and 82. Roster of Confederate Soldiers 1861-1865, Vol. IV, pg. 445. National Archives Catalog ID: 586957, Roll 0047, page 1, Publication number M317.*

Day, Redrick M. (stone reads: R.M. Day MISS)
Corporal, Companies G and F, 13th Regiment Mississippi Infantry
Redrick Day was born in Sumter County, Alabama. He was 20 or 22 years old, a single student and/or a farmer, standing 5 feet 8 inches tall, with dark complexion, dark eyes and black hair. He enlisted in Lauderdale County, Mississippi, to serve for one year. He then traveled 300 miles to muster in at Union City, Tennessee on 4 July 1861. He was appointed Corporal on 2 October 1862. He served at First Manassas, Leesburg, Garnett's Farm, Savage Station, Malvern Hill, Maryland Heights, Sharpsburg, and Fredericksburg. He died of sickness at Fredericksburg on 9 April 1863.
References: *Listed as R.M. Day in the LMA minutes (1888), pages 9 (#133) and 85. Listed as Day, Redrick in the Roster of Confederate Soldiers 1861-1865, Vol. IV, pg. 451. Hodge, "These We Know," pages 43-44. National Archives Catalog ID: 586957, Roll 0215, page 13, Publication number M269.*

Dollar, Willliam (stone reads: Wm Daller ARK)
Private, Company K, 1st Regiment Arkansas Infantry
William Dollar was 25 year old when he enlisted on 8 May 1861 at Little

Rock, Arkansas, to serve for one year. His unit mustered in at Lynchburg, Virginia on 21 May 1861. His service records carry no note of his death, but he is buried in the Fredericksburg City Cemetery.
References: *Recorded as Wm. Daller in the LMA minutes (1888), pages 7 (#76) and 81. Listed as Dollar, William in the Roster of Confederate Soldiers 1861-1865, Vol. V, page 76. Hodge, "These We Know," page 45. National Archives Catalog ID: 586957, Roll 0107, page 3, Publication number M317.*

Duvall, Daniel A. (stone reads: D. Duvall ARK)
Private, Company I, 1st Regiment Arkansas Infantry
Born in Kentucky, this 22 year old carpenter enlisted at Monticello, Arkansas on 8 May 1861, to serve for one year. He mustered into Confederate service at Lynchburg, Virginia on 19 May 1861. His service records give no other information.
References: *LMA minutes (1888), pages 3 (#5) and 83. Roster of Confederate Soldiers 1861-1865, Vol. V, page 215. National Archives Catalog ID: 586957, Roll 0047, page 1, Publication number M 317.*

Edwards, Reuben. J. (stone reads: Reubn J. Edwards ARK)
Private, Company K, 1st Regiment Arkansas Infantry
At the age of 29, this farmer enlisted at Little Rock, Arkansas. He mustered into Confederate service on 21 May 1861 at Lynchburg, Virginia, to serve for the duration of the war. There is no record of how he died.
References: *LMA minutes (1888), pages 5 (#47) and 82. Roster of Confederate Soldiers 1861-1865, Vol. V, page 276. National Archives Catalog ID: 586957, Roll 0047, page 1, Publication number M317.*

Elridge, I. W. (stone reads: Eldridge TENN)
Private, 2nd Regiment Tennessee Infantry
According to the LMA minutes, Eldridge was from Shelbyville, Tennessee and was buried in the grave of B. B. Warwick before being re-interred in the Fredericksburg City Cemetery. This soldier's service records show that he was a Private in the 2nd Tennessee Infantry. His name appears on a record dated 20 May, year not stated, bearing the title "Post register, at Albany, Georgia" with no other information given. There is an F.M. Eldridge who served in Company B, Phillips Georgia Legion who was killed at

Fredericksburg on 13 December 1862. His grave is not on any recorded roster, but the stone could be broken, buried, or the state listed on this stone could be incorrect.

References: *The LMA minutes (1888) record this soldier as Eldridge on pages 9 (#145) and 85. He is listed as Elridge, I. W. in the Roster of Confederate Soldiers 1861-1865, Vol. V, page 324. National Archives Catalog ID: 586957, Roll 0512, page 1, Publication number M266. National Archives Catalog ID 586957, Roll 0594, page 6, Publication number M266.*

Evans, David L. (stone reads: D.L. Evans K 24 GA)
Corporal, Company K, 24th Regiment Georgia Infantry
David Evans enlisted as a Private in 1861, but soon was appointed to the rank of Corporal. His regiment was organized on 24 August 1861 and mustered into Confederate service on 7 September 1861. He spent the period 30 June through 3 September 1862 in the Chimborazo hospitals #2 and #5, in Richmond, Virginia, with a fever. He was killed on 3 May 1863, at Chancellorsville.

References: *LMA minutes (1888), pages 9 (#148) and 85. Roster of Confederate Soldiers 1861-1865, Vol. V, pg. 371. Georgia Roster, Vol. 3, page 83. Hodge, "These We Know," page 50. National Archives Catalog ID: 586957, Roll 0266, page 2, Publication number M 356.*

Everett, Robert (stone reads: R. Everett NC)
Private, Company H, 3rd Regiment North Carolina Infantry (State Troops)
Robert Everett, a 36-year old resident of Bladen County, North Carolina enlisted on 10 May 1861, to serve for the duration of the war. He died of disease in a hospital in Fredericksburg, on 24 October 1861. There is a claim made by Eliza Averitt, widow, filed on 19 September 1862, for the amount of $89.40 in due pay.

References: *LMA minutes (1888), pages 9 (#125) and 85. Roster of Confederate Soldiers 1861-1865, Vol. V, pg. 385. North Carolina Roster Vol. 3, page 570. Hodge, "These We Know," page 50. National Archives Catalog ID: 586957, Roll 0106, page 4, Publication number M 270.*

Farr S. John (stone reads: Jno. Farrs ARK)
Private, Company C, 3rd Regiment Arkansas Infantry
Farr S.J. is recorded as transferring from the 2nd Arkansas Battalion to Company C of the 3rd Arkansas Regiment at Camp Lee, near Petersburg, Virginia, on 18 July 1862, under Special Order No. 152.

Farr also named as Pharr Samuel J., Company C, who was detailed as a nurse at Dumphries, Virginia. In his service record it shows that he was sick on 31 October 1861 yet present in December 1861. His body is buried at the Fredericksburg City Cemetery.

References: Listed as John Farrs in the LMA minutes (1888) pages 7 (#70) and 81. Farr S.J. is in the Roster of Confederate Soldiers 1861-1865, Vol. V, page 423. Pharr, Samuel J. is in the Roster of Confederate Soldiers 1861-1865, Vol. XII, page 305. National Archives Catalog ID: 586957, Roll 0061, page 3, Publication number M317. National Archive Catalog ID: 586957, Roll 0064, page 3, Publication number M317.

There is a John D. Parr (Alabama) buried in the Confederate Cemetery who should not be confused with this soldier.

Fitzgerald, George (stone reads: Geo. Fitzgerald NC)
Private, Company F, 4th Regiment Virginia Light Artillery
George Fitzgerald's stone marker indicates he was from North Carolina, but he joined the Virginia Artillery at Richmond Virginia on 20 April 1861, for one year. He died in a hospital at Fredericksburg, on 13 October 1861.

References: LMA minutes (1888), pages 9 (#127) and 85. Roster of Confederate Soldiers 1861-1865, Vol. IV, page 500. National Archives Catalog ID: 586957, Roll 0277, page 3, Publication number M 324.

Foster, James H. (stone reads: Jas. A. Foster MISS)
Private, Company D, 18th Regiment Mississippi Volunteers
James Foster enlisted on 15 April 1862 at Yazoo City, Mississippi, to serve for three years. From 25 June to September 1862 he was in Richmond, Virginia's Camp Winder Hospital with bronchitis. He was killed at Marye's Hill, at Fredericksburg, on 3 May 1863.

References: Listed as Jas. A. Foster in the LMA minutes (1888), pages 9 (#131) and 85. Listed as Foster, James H. in the Roster of Confederate Soldiers 1861-1865, Vol. VI, page 74. Hodge, "These We Know," page 54. National Archives Catalog ID: 586957, Roll 0267, page 8, Publication number M269.

French, Walter Y. (stone reads: Walter French ARK)
Sergeant, Company D, 1st Regiment Arkansas Infantry
French was 24 years old when he enlisted at Pine Bluff, Arkansas on 1 May 1861, with the rank of Sergeant. He was a mechanic by trade and agreed to serve for one year. His service record contains a notation that he was sick in camp, but with no date or location.
References: LMA minutes (1888), pages 5 (# 63) and 82. Roster of Confederate Soldiers 1861-1865, Vol. VI, page 134. Hodge, "These We Know," page 55. National Archives Catalog ID: 586957, Roll 0047, page 3, Publication number M317.

Gaddy, Clem (stone reads: Clem Paddy NC)
Private, Company K, 22nd Regiment North Carolina Infantry (formerly 12th North Carolina Infantry, Volunteers)
Clem Gaddy, a 34 year old resident of McDowell County, North Carolina enlisted on 24 July 1861, in Raleigh, North Carolina, for one year. On 25 August 1861, he was recorded absent sick and sent to Fredericksburg, Virginia, where he later died of disease on 10 October 1861. His wife, Rachel M. Gaddy, filed a claim on 17 December 1864.
References: Listed as Clem Paddy in the LMA minutes (1888), pages 3 (#31) and 83. Listed as Gatty, Clem in the Roster of Confederate Soldiers 1861-1865, Vol. VI, page 178. National Archives Catalog ID: 586957, Roll 0287, page 8, Publication number M270.

Gardiner, Cosley W. (stone reads: Cosley Gardner NC)
Corporal, Company G, 1st Regiment North Carolina Infantry
Cosley Gardiner was a resident of Washington County, North Carolina when he enlisted at Plymouth on 24 June 1861, at the age of 24. He mustered into Confederate service as a Corporal and died at Brooke Station, Virginia on 11 October 1861.
References: Listed as Cosley Gardner in the LMA minutes (1888), pages 11 (#165) and 84. Listed as Gardiner, C.W. in the Roster of Confederate Soldiers 1861-1865, Vol. VI, page 207. North Carolina Roster, Vol. 3, page 215. Hodge, "These We Know," page 56. National Archives Catalog ID: 586957, Roll 0093, page 4, Publication number M 270.

Gatewood, John Dudley (stone reads: John Gatewood NC)
Private, Company H, 22nd Regiment North Carolina Infantry (formerly 12th North Carolina Infantry, Volunteers)
John Gatewood was 25 years old when he enlisted in Stokes County, North Carolina on 1 June 1861, to serve for one year. He was paid a bounty of $10. On 19 August 1861, he was reported as being sick at Fredericksburg, Virginia, where he died of disease in October.
References: *LMA minutes (1888), pages 3 (#1) and 83. Roster of Confederate Soldiers 1861-1865, Vol. VI, page 248. Hodge, "These We Know," page 58. National Archives Catalog ID: 586957, Roll 0287, page 3, Publication number M 270.*

Gatewood, William (stone reads: W. Gatewood NC)
Private, Company H, 22nd Regiment North Carolina Infantry (formerly 12 North Carolina Infantry, Volunteers)
William Gatewood was 25 years old when he was paid a bounty of $10 for enlisting in Stokes County, North Carolina on 1 June 1861, to serve for one year. He was reported sick at Fredericksburg Virginia and died of disease there on 11 September 1861. He was buried by William H. Norton, who submitted a bill of $15 for the burial of soldiers who died at Hospital # 2 in Fredericksburg. George Gatewood, not identified, but perhaps William Gatewood's father, filed a settlement claim on 14 November 1862.
References: *LMA minutes (1888), pages 3 (#24) and 83. Roster of Confederate Soldiers 1861-1865, Vol. VI, page 249. Hodge, "These We Know," page 58. National Archives Catalog ID: 586957, Roll 0287, page 3, Publication number M270.*

Gerrell, A. F. (stone reads: D. Grinnell NC)
Private, Company I, 22nd Regiment North Carolina Infantry (State Troops)
The LMA minutes record Grinnell as a soldier in the 12th North Carolina Infantry, but there was no one in that unit by that name. The 12th Regiment North Carolina Infantry (Volunteers) became the 22nd Regiment North Carolina Infantry (State Troops) on 14 November 1861, but there is no one with the name Grinnell in that unit either. A possible match for this soldier could be A. F. Gerrell, who was wounded, place not stated, whose name is also spelled A. F. Jarrell. He died at the age of 23 in February of 1862.

There is also a soldier named M. D. Grinnell found in A. E. Small's personal records, Lt., Ord. Office dated January 1863, index card (382)

6660. Small was assigned to Company F, 11th North Carolina Infantry. No other information given.
References: *LMA minutes (1888), pages 3 (#11) and 83. Gerrell, A. F. is found in the Roster of Confederate Soldiers 1861-1865, Vol. VI, page 277. National Archives Catalog ID: 2133276, Roll 0159, page 1, Publication number M 347. National Archives Catalog ID: 586957, Roll 0287, page 2, Publication number M 270. National Archives Catalog ID: 586957, Roll 0288, page 6, Publication number M 270.*

Green, Edward (stone reads: Edward Greer NC)
Private, Company E, 3rd Regiment North Carolina Infantry (State Troops)
Edward Green was a resident of Onslow County when he enlisted on 13 May 1861, at the age of 21. He mustered into Confederate service the same day. Green died in a hospital at Fredericksburg, on 27 October 1861.
References: *Listed as Edward Greer in the LMA minutes (1888), pages 9 (#123) and 84. Listed as Green, Edward in the Roster of Confederate Soldiers 1861-1865, Vol. VI, page 472. National Archives Catalog ID: 586957, Roll 0126, page 3, Publication number M 270.*

Green, Joseph (stone reads: Jos. Greer NC)
Private, Company I, 2nd Regiment North Carolina Infantry (State Troops)
Joseph Green was a 22 year old resident of Craven County, North Carolina when he enlisted on 29 May 1861 at New Berne, North Carolina. He mustered into Confederate service the same day. Green died on 24 October 1861, at Camp Potomac, Virginia.
References: *Listed as Jos. Greer in the LMA minutes (1888), pages 9 (#124) and 84. Listed as Green, Joseph in the Roster of Confederate Soldiers 1861-1865, Vol. VI, page 480. National Archives Catalog ID: 586957, Roll 0109, page 6, Publication number M 270.*

Griffin, Levi (stone reads: Levi Griffin NC)
Private, Company F, 2nd Regiment North Carolina Infantry (State Troops)
Levi Griffin was a resident of Craven County, North Carolina, when he enlisted there, at the age of 18, on 27 May 1861. He mustered into Confederate service the same day. He died of disease on 15 August 1861 in Fredericksburg, Virginia.
References: *LMA minutes (1888), pages 5 (#55) and 82. Roster of Confederate*

Soldiers 1861-1865, Vol. VII, page 15. National Archives Catalog ID: 586957, Roll 0109, page 2, Publication number M270.

A stone marker was placed at Griffin's grave site on 29 March 2008 by the Matthew Fontaine Maury Camp 1722.

Hanes, James K. (stone reads: J. Harrer TENN)
Private, Company D, 1st Regiment Tennessee Infantry
There is no one listed in any Tennessee Regiment named Harrer. A likely match for this soldier is James K. Hanes. Hanes enlisted on 27 April 1862 at Yorktown, Virginia. He was sworn into service by Captain Awalt for two years. His service record shows that he was killed at Spotsylvania Court House, on 10 May 1864.
References: *J. Harrer is listed in the LMA minutes (1888), pages 5 (#59) and 82. Hanes James K. is listed in the Roster of Confederate Soldiers 1861-1865, Vol. VII, page 186. National Archives Catalog ID: 586957, Roll 0108, page 12, Publication number M268.*

Hardin, Samuel L. (new stone reads: S.L. Harden MISS)
Private, Company K, 17th Regiment Mississippi Volunteers
On 28 May 1861 Harden traveled 122 miles to enlist at Corinth, Mississippi, to serve for 12 months. He was 22 years old, born in Georgia, and a farmer by trade. Hardin was killed in action at Fredericksburg on 11 December 1862.
References: *Listed as S.L. Harden in the LMA minutes (1888), pages 11 (#177) and 85. Listed as Harding, Samuel L. in the Roster of Confederate Soldiers 1861-1865, Vol. VII, page 215. National Archives Catalog ID: 586957, Roll 0213, page 13, Publication number M269.*
The Matthew Fontaine Maury Camp 1722 of the Sons of Confederate Veterans placed a new marker on 29 March 2008.

Harrell, Edward (stone reads: Harrell TENN)
Corporal, Company F, 2nd Regiment Tennessee Infantry
Edward Harrell enlisted at Millersburg, Tennessee on 25 April 1861. He was 27 years old and agreed to serve for one year when he mustered into Confederate service. His death was originally recorded on 30 July 1861, but his service record shows him dying on 9 August 1861 at Fredericksburg, Virginia.
References: *LMA minutes (1888), pages 5 (#53) and 82. Roster of Confederate*

Soldiers 1861-1865, Vol. VII, page 254. National Archives Catalog ID: 586957, Roll 0115, page 4, Publication number M268

Harrison S.C. (stone reads: J.C. Handison ARK)
Private, Company H, 1ˢᵗ Regiment Arkansas Infantry
There is no one named J.C. Handison found in any Arkansas unit. There is, however, a soldier named Harrison, S.C. who was found sick at Dumphries, Virginia in November of 1861, which fits this soldier's profile and places him near Fredericksburg.
References: *Listed as J.C. Handison in the LMA minutes (1888), pages 7 (#78) and 81. Listed as Harrison, S. C. in the Roster of Confederate Soldiers 1861-1865, Vol. VII, page 302. National Archives Catalog ID: 586957, Roll 0048, page 3, Publication number M317.*

Heath, Joseph H. (stone reads: Jas. H. Heath TENN)
Private, Company G, 2ⁿᵈ Regiment Tennessee Infantry
On 25 April 1861, a 24 year old Joseph Heath enlisted in Nashville, Tennessee, for 3 years. He mustered into Confederate service on 17 May 1861 in Lynchburg Virginia. He died in Virginia (date not stated) and is buried in Fredericksburg.
References: *Listed as Jas. H. Heath in the LMA minutes (1888), pages 7 (#80) and 81. Listed as Heath, Joseph H. in the Roster of Confederate Soldiers 1861-1865, Vol. VII, page 456. National Archives Catalog ID: 586957, Roll 0115, page 1, Publication number M268.*

Henderson, James B. (stone reads: J.B. Henderson NC)
Private, Company G, 3ʳᵈ Regiment North Carolina Infantry (State Troops)
This 23 year old man enlisted at Jacksonville, North Carolina, on 1 July 1861, to serve for the duration of the war. He died on 27 August or 1 September 1861 in a hospital in Fredericksburg, Virginia. Among his effects was recorded $15.50.
References: *LMA minutes (1888), pages 5 (#41) and 82. Roster of Confederate Soldiers 1861-1865, Vol. VII, page 427. Hodge, "These We Know," page 69. National Archives Catalog ID: 586957, Roll 0127, page 3, Publication number M270.*

Henry, Thomas J. (stone: T.F. Henry ARK)
Private, Company D, 1st Regiment Arkansas Infantry
Born in Fayette County, Arkansas, Thomas Henry was the son of John G. Henry. At the age of 20 or 21, he enlisted on 1 May 1861 at Pine Bluff, Arkansas, for one year. His unit mustered into Confederate service at Lynchburg, Virginia on 19 May 1861. His service record does not indicate when he died, but he was noted to be sick in a hospital in Fredericksburg, Virginia and his father made a claim for his effects on 24 March 1862.
References: *Listed as T.F. Henry in the LMA minutes (1888), pages 7 (#83) and 81. Listed as Henry, T.J. in the Roster of Confederate Soldiers 1861-1865, Vol. VII, page 456. Hodge, "These We Know," page 70. National Archives Catalog ID: 586957, Roll 0048, page 5, Publication number M317.*
When Thomas Henry's father filed a claim for his son's effects on 24 March 1862, he also filed a claim for the effects of his other son, Isaac F. Henry, who had also died in Fredericksburg at or around the same time as his brother.

Hicks, Stephen L. (stone reads: S.L. Hicks ARK)
Private, Company I, 1st Regiment Arkansas Infantry
This 24 year old carpenter enlisted on 8 May 1861 at Monticello, Arkansas, to serve for a period of one year. He mustered into Confederate service on 19 May 1861, at Lynchburg, Virginia. His service record does not record his death, but he is buried in Fredericksburg.
References: *LMA minutes (1888), pages 7 (#68) and 81. Roster of Confederate Soldiers 1861-1865, Vol. VII, page 506. Hodge, "These We Know," page 71. National Archives Catalog ID: 586957, Roll 0048, page 3, Publication number M317.*

Higgins, Newton (stone reads: Newton Higgen GA)
Private, Company C, 24th Regiment Georgia Infantry
Newton was a resident of White County, Georgia when he enlisted on 24 August 1861, for the duration of the war. He mustered into Confederate service the same day. He was killed on 3 May 1863, at Chancellorsville.
References: *Listed as Newton Higgen in the LMA minutes (1888), pages 7 (#101) and 84. Listed as Newton Higgins in the Roster of Confederate soldiers 1861-1865, Vol. VII, page 514. National Archives Catalog ID: 586957, Roll 0357, page 5, Publication number M 266.*

Holloway, N. A. (stone reads: Hollaway NC)
Private, Company A, 22nd Regiment North Carolina Infantry (formerly 12th North Carolina Infantry Volunteers)
Holloway was 23 years old when he collected a bounty of $10 for enlisting at Lenoir, North Carolina on 30 April 1861, to serve for one year. He was sick in Fredericksburg, Virginia in August 1861 and died of disease on 13 or 21 September 1861.
References: *Hollaway is listed in the LMA minutes (1888), pages 3 (#18) and 83. Listed as Holloway, N. A. in the Roster of Confederate Soldiers 1861-1865, Vol. VIII, page 118. Hodge, "These We Know," page 73. National Archives Catalog ID: 586957, Roll 0288, page 2, Publication number M270.*

Hubbard, Josiah (stone reads: Jos. Hubbard NC)
Private, Company I, 1st Regiment North Carolina Infantry (State Troops)
Josiah Hubbard was a 25 year old resident of Wake County, North Carolina, when he enlisted there on 16 July 1861. He mustered into Confederate service on 20 July 1861. Hubbard died of unknown causes on 19 September 1861, in Fredericksburg.
References: *LMA minutes (1888), pages 3 (#10) and 83. Roster of Confederate Soldiers 1861-1865, Vol. VIII, page 215. National Archives Catalog ID: 586957, Roll 0094, page 3, Publication number M 270.*

Hubbert M. M. (stone reads: M.M. Herbert MISS)
Private, Company I, 13th Regiment Mississippi Infantry
On 13 May 1861, Hubbert had traveled 200 miles to enlist at Corinth Mississippi, for one year. He was 23 years old. On 1 December 1861, Hubbert was transferred to the regimental band. He was promoted to Sergeant on 8 November 1862. He died in Fredericksburg, on 18 April 1863.
References: *Listed as M.M. Herbert in the LMA minutes (1888), pages 9 (#132) and 85. Listed as Hubbert, M. M. in the Roster of Confederate Soldiers 1861-1865, Vol. VIII, page 217. National Archives Catalog ID: 586957, Roll 0215, page 20, Publication number M269.*

Jarrell, James (stone reads: Jas. Jerrold NC)
Private, Company E, 1st Regiment North Carolina Infantry
Jarrell was 23 years old when he enlisted on 8 June 1861 at Wilmington,

North Carolina, to serve for the duration of the war. He died of disease prior to 31 August 1861.
References: *Listed as Jas. Jerrold in the LMA minutes (1888) pages 3 (#8) and 83. Listed as Jarrell, James in the Roster of Confederate Soldiers 1861-1865, Vol. VIII, page 400. Hodge, "These We Know," page 79. National Archives Catalog ID: 586957, Roll 0094, pages 2-3, Publication number M 270.*

Johnson, William Howell (stone reads: Wm. H. Johnson ARK)
Private, Company I, 1ˢᵗ Regiment Arkansas Infantry
This 21 year old clerk enlisted at Monticello, Arkansas on May 1861. He was mustered into the Confederate service at Lynchburg, Virginia on 19 May 1861. His service record contains no other information.
References: *LMA minutes (1888), pages 7 (#81) and 81. Roster of Confederate Soldiers 1861-1865, Vol. VIII, page 499. Hodge, "These We Know." page 81. National Archives Catalog ID: 586957, Roll 0048, page 3, Publication number M317.*

Joyce, George W. (stone reads: Geo. W. Joice NC)
Private, Company H, 12ᵗʰ Regiment North Carolina Infantry, Volunteers
Joyce was a resident of Stokes County, North Carolina, when he enlisted in Danbury, North Carolina on 1 June 1861, for one year. His service record shows that he was sick at Fredericksburg, Virginia on 29 August 1861. He died of disease, at the age of 19, on 24 October 1861 and his effects were distributed among his friends in the Company, at the request of Hamilton Joyce, his father. There is a note that $15 was paid to William H. Norton for burial of Soldiers at No. 3 Hospital, Fredericksburg, Virginia, on 25 October 1861.
References: *Geo. W. Joice is recorded in the LMA minutes (1888), pages 11 (#161) and 84. Listed as Joyce, George W. in the Roster of Confederate Soldiers 1861-1865, Vol. IX, page 43. National Archives Catalog ID: 586957, Roll 0288, page 6, Publication number M 270.*

Lackey, Edward (stone reads: Edwd. Letty NC)
Private, Company E, 12ᵗʰ North Carolina Infantry (State Troops)
Edward Lackey lived in Cleveland County, North Carolina and enlisted to serve for one year. He was 24 years old and mustered into Confederate service at Shelby, North Carolina on 6 October 1861. Lackey was mortally wounded at Chancellorsville, on 2 May 1863 and died 8 May 1863.

References: Edward Letty is recorded in the LMA minutes (1888), pages 5 (#60) and 82. Lackey, Edward J. is listed in the Roster of Confederate Soldiers 1861-1865, Vol. IX, page 262. National Archives Catalog ID: 586957, Roll 0051, page 4, Publication number M317

Lackey, William (stone reads: Wm. Lackey NC)
Private, Company K, 22nd Regiment North Carolina Infantry (formerly 12th Regiment North Carolina Infantry, Volunteers)
At the age of 17, William Lackey enlisted in Wake County, North Carolina. He was a resident of McDowell County, North Carolina. He mustered into Confederate service on 5 June 1861 and died of disease on 8 October 1861 at Fredericksburg, Virginia.
References: LMA minutes (1888), pages 3 (#14) and 83. Roster of Confederate Soldiers 1861-1865, Vol. IX, page 263. National Archives Catalog ID: 586957, Roll 0289, page 5, Publication number M 270.
    On 29 March 2008, the Matthew Fontaine Maury Camp 1722 placed a marker in memory of this soldier.

Laymon, William P. (stone reads: W.P. Layman ARK)
Private, Company E, 1st Regiment Arkansas Infantry
This 20 year old farmer enlisted at Benton, Arkansas on 25 April 1861, to serve for one year. He mustered into Confederate service on 19 May 1861, at Lynchburg, Virginia. His service record contains no other information.
References: Listed as W.P. Layman in the LMA minutes (1888), pages 5 (#65) and 82. Listed as Laymon, William P. in the Roster of Confederate Soldiers 1861-1865, Vol. IX, page 368. National Archives Catalog ID: 586957, Roll 0049, page 1, Publication number M317.

Leech, William H.H. (stone reads: W.K. Leach ARK)
Private, Company E, 1st Regiment Arkansas Infantry
William Leach was a 21 year old farmer when he enlisted on 26 April 1861 at Benton, Arkansas, to serve for one year. The record shows $15 paid to William H. Horton on 24 September 1861, to bury this soldier near Hospital No. 2 in Fredericksburg. His body was later reinterred in the Fredericksburg City Cemetery.
References: Listed as W.K. Leach in the LMA minutes (1888), pages 3 (#7) and 83. Listed as Leach, William H.H. in the Roster of Confederate Soldiers

1861-1865, Vol. IX, page 406. National Archives Catalog ID: 586957, Roll 0049, page 4, Publication number M 317.

Lewis, Francis P. (stone reads: Francis Lewis NC)
Private, Company G, 1ˢᵗ Regiment North Carolina Infantry (State Troops)
Lewis Francis, at the age of 23, enlisted on 22 July 1861, to serve for the duration of the war. He was from Washington County, North Carolina. His service record shows that he died on 12 October 1861 at Brooke Station, Stafford County, Virginia.
References: *LMA minutes (1888), pages 11 (#164) and 85. National Archives Catalog ID: 586957, Roll 0095 page 4, Publication number M 270.*

Liverman, Frederick (stone reads: F. Liverman NC)
Private, Company G, 1ˢᵗ Regiment North Carolina Infantry
Frederick Liverman resided in Washington County, North Carolina, where he enlisted on 29 June 1861, to serve for the duration of the war. He was 36 years old and signed with his mark. He died of disease on 20 October 1861, at Brooke Station, Stafford County, Virginia.
References: *LMA minutes (1888), pages 11 (#163) and 83. Roster of Confederate Soldiers 1861-1865, Vol. IX, page 506. North Carolina Roster, Vol. 3, page 217. Hodge, "These We Know," page 88. National Archives Catalog ID: 586957, Roll 0095, page 3, Publication number M 270.*

Luster, Morgan (stone reads: Morgan Luster ARK)
Private, Company H, 39ᵗʰ Regiment, Tennessee Mounted Infantry
Luster, Morgan M. is recorded in The Roster of Confederate Soldiers as serving in the 39ᵗʰ Regiment, Tennessee Mounted Infantry, Company H. His service record shows that he joined Colonel W. M Bradford's regiment of volunteers on 19 March 1861, for one year. There is a record of Luster in the National Archives showing that he served as an Arkansas soldier, but there is no reference to a unit. The LMA minutes also note that Luster was from Arkansas. Luster's service record notes that he was found absent without leave, with no date given. Morgan Luster also appears on an account dated 24 June 1861, in the amount of $15, for the burial of soldiers at Hospital No. 1 in Fredericksburg by William H. Norton.
References: *The LMA minutes (1888), pages 7 (#89) and 81, indicate Luster was from Arkansas. He is identified as serving in the 39ᵗʰ Regiment Tennessee Mounted Infantry in the Roster of Confederate Soldiers 1861-1865, Vol. X, page*

84. National Archives Catalog ID: 586957, Roll 0243, page 1, Publication number M347. National Archives Catalog ID: 586957, Roll 0297, pages 1-3, Publication number M268.

Lynch, Henry N. (stone reads: H.N. Lynch D2 GA)
Private, Company D, 2nd Regiment Georgia Infantry
Henry Lynch enlisted in Muscogee County, Georgia on 20 June 1861. He died in a Fredericksburg hospital on 3 September 1861. There was a claim made by his mother Elizabeth Lynch, on 19 July 1862, in the amount of $55.66.
References: *LMA minutes (1888), pages 3 (#33) and 82. Roster of Confederate Soldiers 1861-1865, Vol. X, page 91. Georgia Roster, Vol. 1, page 397. Hodge, "These We Know," page 89. National Archives Catalog ID: 586957, Roll 0154, page 5, Publication number M270.*

Lynch, William C. (stone reads: Wm. C. Lynch TENN)
Private, Company F, 2nd Regiment Tennessee Infantry
William Lynch enlisted on 25 April or 1 May 1861 at Millersburg, Tennessee. He was 25 or 26 years old and planned to serve only one year. His regiment was organized and mustered into Confederate service on 6 May 1861. Company records compiled 24 July 1863 record that he died on 9 June 1861.
References: *LMA minutes (1888), pages 7 (#93) and 81. Roster of the Confederate Soldiers 1861-1865, Vol. X, page 94. Hodge, "These We Know," page 90. National Archives Catalog ID: 586957, Roll 0116, page 3, Publication number M268.*

Marbang Sevear (stone reads: Sevear Marbang ARK)
Private, 1st Regiment Arkansas Infantry
Sevear Marbang is recorded in the LMA minutes (1888) Register page 9 (#129) as a soldier who served in the 1st Arkansas Regiment as a Private. There is no other information found on this soldier, but his name is strikingly similar to the next entry. This name is not in The Roster of Confederate Soldiers 1861-1865. If this name is not correct, however, the question is who is in the grave?

Marbury, Sevier (stone reads: Sev. Moulbry ARK)
Private, Company B, 1ˢᵗ Regiment Arkansas Infantry
Sevier Marbury was born in 1843. He was an 18 years old student who enlisted at Little Rock, Arkansas on 8 May 1861. There are no other records of him found after 19 May 1861.
References: *He is listed at Sev. Moulbry in the LMA minutes (1888), pages 9 (#129) and 85. He is listed as Marbury, Sevier P. in the Roster of Confederate Soldiers 1861-1865, Vol. X, page 166. National Archives Catalog ID: 586957, Roll 0049, page 1, Publication number M 317. There is no entry for the name Moulbry in The Roster of Confederate Soldiers 1861-1865.*

Marchman, Stephen, R. (new stone reads: Stephen R. Marchman ARK)
Private, Company B, 1ˢᵗ Regiment Arkansas Infantry
This 18 or 19 year old farmer enlisted on 19 May 1861 at Little Rock or Arkadelphia, Arkansas and mustered into Confederate service at Lynchburg, Virginia. He died in a hospital at Fredericksburg, Virginia on 28 June 1861.
References: *The 1888 LMA Register recorded Marchman's name in the Fredericksburg Cemetery, next to the stone of William C. Lynch (page 81). Listed as Marchman, Stephen R. in the Roster of Confederate Soldiers 1861-1865 Vol. X, page 168. Hodge, "These We Know," page 92. National Archives Catalog ID; 586957, Roll 0049, page 3, Publication number M 317.*

On 25 May 2006 the Matthew Fontaine Maury Camp 1722 placed a headstone marker at Marchman's grave site.

Mashburn John (stone reads: J. Mashman NC)
Private, Company G, 3ʳᵈ Regiment North Carolina Infantry (State Troops)
On 1 July 1861, John Mashburn enlisted at Jacksonville, North Carolina. On 1 August 1861, he was recorded absent, sick at Hospital No. 1 in Fredericksburg, Virginia. He died there on 1 September 1861.
References: *Listed as J. Mashman in the LMA minutes (1888), pages 5 (#39) and 82. Listed as Mashburn, John in the Roster of Confederate Soldiers 1861-1865, Vol. X, page 232. National Archives Catalog ID: 586957, Roll 0129, page 5, Publication number M270.*

McAdams, James O.A. (stone missing)
Private, Company A, 1st Regiment Arkansas Infantry)
The LMA minutes show this soldier serving in Company A, 24th Georgia Infantry, with no other information. The stone marker, however, states that he was from Arkansas. Although James McAdams is not a conclusive match for this soldier he best fits the given information.

James McAdams, a farmer by trade, enlisted on 2 May 1861, at El Dorado, Arkansas. He mustered into Confederate service on 19 May 1861, at Lynchburg, Virginia. He died of disease on 13 November 1861, in Fredericksburg.
References: *LMA minutes (1888), pages 7 (#102) and 84. Listed as McAdams, James O.A. in the Roster of Confederate Soldiers 1861-1865, Vol. X, page 304. National Archives Catalog ID: 586957, Roll 0049, page 5, Publication number M 317.*

McCance, Robert (stone reads: Robt McCance ARK)
Private, Company D, 1st Regiment Arkansas Infantry
Robert McCance was 27 year old farmer when he enlisted on 1 May 1861, at Pine Bluff, Arkansas, to serve for one year. His name appears on the accounts of William H. Norton, undertaker, dated 14 September 1861, for the burial of soldiers from Hospital #2 in Fredericksburg, Virginia.
References: *LMA minutes (1888), pages 3 (#19) and 83. Roster of Confederate Soldiers 1861-1865, Vol. X, page 329. Hodge, "These We Know," pages 95-96. National Archives Catalog ID: 586957, Roll 0049, page 3, Publication number M317.*

McKie, William (stone reads: McKee MISS)
2nd Lieutenant, Company C, 18th Regiment Mississippi Volunteers
This 27 year old married farmer traveled 236 miles from Canton, Mississippi, to enlist at Corinth, Mississippi on 28 May 1861, to serve for one year. He was promoted to Sergeant in August 1861 and reenlisted at Lee's Mills, Virginia on 15 February 1862 to serve two more years or for the duration of the war. He was elected to the rank of Lieutenant on 30 April 1862. He died on 24 May 1863 of wounds received at Fredericksburg on 3 May 1863.
References: *Listed as McKee in the LMA minutes (1888), pages 11 (#188) and 86. Listed as McKie, William in the Roster of Confederate Soldiers 1861-1865, Vol. X, page 499. Hodge, "These We Know," page 97. National Archives Catalog ID: 586957, Roll 0271, page 8, Publication number M 229.*

McRae, David B. (stone reads: David McCrey VA)
Private, Company B, 13th Regiment Mississippi Volunteers
David McRae was born in Mississippi. He was a 22 year old farmer living near Waynesboro, Mississippi, when he enlisted on 14 May 1861 at Corinth, to serve for one year. He was sick in the General Hospital at Leesburg, Virginia from 2-5 December 1861 and at Chimborazo Hospital #3 in Richmond, Virginia from 16-26 January 1862. He died of disease at Fredericksburg, Virginia on 3 March 1863.
References: Listed as David McCrey in the LMA minutes (1888), pages 9 (#137) and 85. Listed as McRae, David B. in the Roster of Confederate Soldiers 1861-1865, Vol. XI, page 29. Hodge, "These We Know," page 98. National Archives Catalog ID: 586957, Roll 0216, page 19, Publication number M269.

McRoberts, Robert (stone reads: Robt McRoberts ARK)
Private, Company C, 1st Regiment Arkansas Infantry
Joseph McRoberts, of Calhoun County, Arkansas filed a settlement claim on 4 August 1862 asking for the pay due his son from 19 May to 20 July 1862. The latter date is when his son died at Fredericksburg, Virginia. The amount sought was $47.73.
References: LMA minutes (1888), pages 5 (#67) and 82. Roster of Confederate Soldiers 1861-1865, Vol. XI, page 33. Hodge, "These We Know," page 98. National Archives Catalog ID: 586957, Roll 0049, page 8, Publication number M317.

Miller, Ezekiel P. (stone missing)
Lieutenant, Company K, 17th Regiment Mississippi Infantry
Ezekiel Miller was a 23 year old single student, born in South Carolina, living in Paris, Mississippi, when he traveled 122 miles to enlist on 28 May 1861, at Corinth, Mississippi, to serve for one year. He was appointed a Sergeant on 15 October 1861 and in August of 1862 received his bounty for reenlisting. He was elected Lieutenant on 10 or 20 November 1862 and was killed at Fredericksburg on 11 December 1862. His father, M.T. Miller, filed a settlement claim for Ezekiel P. and for William T. Miller, the latter killed on 24 June 1862 in Richmond Virginia.
References: LMA minutes (1888), pages 11 (#178) and 85. Roster of Confederate Soldiers 1861-1865, Vol. XI, page 117. Hodge, "These We Know," pages 98-99. National Archives Catalog ID: 586957, Roll 0257, page 12, Publication number M269.

Miller, Joseph A. (stone missing)
Private, Company K, 17th Regiment Mississippi Infantry
This 18 year old single farmer, born in South Carolina, but residing in Paris, Mississippi, enlisted at Sarepta, Mississippi on 12 March 1862, to serve for three years. He was killed on 3 May 1863, at the second battle of Fredericksburg.
References: *LMA minutes (1888), pages 11 (#181) and 86, where he is listed as having a marble tombstone. Roster of Confederate Soldiers 1861-1865, Vol. XI, page 131. Hodge, "These We Know," page 99. National Archives Catalog ID: 586957, Roll 0257, page 8, Publication number M269.*

Millsaps, Duncan G.C. (stone reads: Dr. Millsops ARK)
Private, Company D, 1st Regiment Arkansas Infantry
This 31 year old farmer enlisted 1 May 1861 at Pine Bluff, Arkansas to serve for one year. He died in Hospital #1 at Fredericksburg, Virginia. His name appears as Doct. Millsaps on the Account rendered by William H. Norton, undertaker, who was paid $15 for the burial of the dead from Fredericksburg hospitals.
References: *Listed in the LMA minutes (1888) as Dr. Millsaps on page 3 (#22) and as Millsops on page 83. Roster of Confederate Soldiers 1861-1865, Vol. XI, page 155. Hodge, "These We Know," page 99. National Archives Catalog ID: 586957, Roll 0050, page 8, Publication number M317.*

Moore, Horace (stone reads: Horace Moore ARK)
Private, Arkansas
References: *LMA minutes (1888), pages 7 (#82) and 81. His name is listed as "Horace Morre" and is referred to as an Indian. In the Internment Register, 1844-1961, page 8, prepared by Robert A. Hodge, Moore is referenced as an "Arkansas Indian soldier that fell at Fredericksburg, Va. and nursed by L. McGrath." According to the 1860 Census, Loretta McGrath, age 30, was a school teacher by profession who lived in Fredericksburg, Virginia.*

Moss, William (stone reads: Mose VA)
Private, Company D, 40th Virginia Infantry
William Moss enlisted at Heathsville, Virginia on 1 March 1861. Although his service records do not indicate that he died in Fredericksburg, it does show that he was sick in April of 1862. The 40th Virginia was unattached

between April and May of 1862, at the Aquia District, Department of Northern Virginia. It was then assigned to Field's Brigade, A. P. Hills Division, Army of the Northern Virginia, which places him at or near Fredericksburg.
References: Listed as Mose in the LMA minutes (1888), pages 5 (#37) and 82. Listed as Moss, William in the Roster of Confederate Soldiers 1861-1865, Vol. XI, page 352. National Archives Catalog ID: 586957, Roll 0857, page 3, Publication number M327.

Myers, Felix (stone reads: Fred Myer ARK)
Private, Company B, 14th Regiment North Carolina Infantry (State Troops)
There is no reference to a Fred Myer in any Arkansas Regiment, but there is a Felix Myers, which fits this soldier's profile. On 16 July 1862, Felix Myers, a resident of Davidson County, North Carolina, enlisted in Wake County, North Carolina. He mustered into Confederate service on 16 July 1862. He was killed on 3 May 1863 at Chancellorsville.
References: Listed as Fred Myer in the LMA minutes (1888), pages 7 (#85) and 81. Listed as Myers, Felix in the Roster of Confederate Soldiers 1861-1865, Vol. XI, page 417. National Archives Catalog ID: 586957, Roll 0227, page 5, Publication number M270

O'Donnell, Michael (stone reads: Mike O'Donnell ARK)
Private, Company F, 1st Regiment Arkansas Infantry
 O'Donnell was a 24 or 25 year old laborer who enlisted at Little Rock, Arkansas, on 8 May 1861 and mustered into Confederate service at Lynchburg, Virginia, on 19 May 1861. He was sick at a hospital in Fredericksburg, Virginia on 29 June 1861, but his service record does not record his death.
References: LMA minutes (1888), pages 5 (#52) and 82. Roster of Confederate Soldiers 1861-1865, Vol. XII, page 23. Hodge, "These We Know," page 105. National Archives Catalog ID: 586957, Roll 0050, page 3, Publication number M317.

Old, John N. (stone reads: J.M. Old MISS)
Private, Virginia Light Artillery
John Old is recorded in the LMA minutes as serving in a Mississippi unit, but there is no one by that name on any Mississippi unit roster. A likely

match for this soldier is John Nelson Old, who served in the Charlottesville Light Artillery.

Old was born in Albemarle County, Virginia and enlisted on 15 March 1862, to serve for the duration of the war. He died in Fredericksburg, Virginia on 12 May 1864 from wounds received in action.

References: *Listed as J.M. Old in the LMA minutes (1888), pages 11 (#189) and 86. Listed as Old, John N. in the Roster of Confederate Soldiers 1861-1865, Vol. XII, page 33. National Archives Catalog ID: 586957, Roll 0272, page 12, Publication number M 324.*

Oliver, Henry B. (stone reads: N.P. Oliver NC)
Private, Company D, 1st Regiment Texas Infantry
While records within the packet of this man contain the correct name, Henry P. Oliver. The listing in the index and main jacket of the Compiled Service Records name him as H.B. Oliver. He enrolled from Cass County, Texas on May 26, 1861 to serve for one year. He died of pneumonia in a Fredericksburg, Virginia hospital on March 28, 1862. His father, Samuel Oliver, filed a settlement claim on 6 December 1862, which was approved for payment on 8 December 1862. The claim was for pay from 1 November 1861 to 28 March 1862 (4 months 28 days, at $11 per month.) The $83.26 paid included $54.26 for that period and also $29 for clothing allowance. There is a note that there is further information on this man among the personal papers of Private John A. Oliver, Company D, 1st Texas Infantry. Private Oliver appears with the initials N.P. in some records and is sometimes referenced as being from North Carolina.

References: *Listed as N.P. Oliver in the LMA minutes (1888), pages 11 (#167) and 85. Listed as Oliver, H.B. in the Roster of Confederate Soldiers 1861-1865, Vol. XII, page 39. Hodge, "These We Know," page 106. National Archives Catalog ID: 586957, Roll 0253, page 4, Publication number M323.*

Oliver, John A. (stone reads: John A. Oliver TEX)
Private, Company D, 1st Regiment Texas Infantry
This company was organized in Marion County, Texas and mustered into Confederate service at New Orleans Louisiana, on 6 June 1861. John Oliver died of pneumonia in a Fredericksburg, hospital on 1 April 1862.

References: *LMA minutes (1888), pages 9 (#130) and 85. Roster of Confederate Soldiers 1861-1865, Vol. XII, page 40. Texas Roster, page 36.*

Hodge, "These We Know," page 106. National Archives Catalog ID: 586957, Roll 0253, page 4, Publication number M323

Overstreet, Christenbury C. (stone reads: C.C. Overstreet ARK)
Private, Company C, 1ˢᵗ Regiment Arkansas Infantry
This 34 year old overseer enlisted on 8 May 1861, at Camden, Arkansas, to serve for one year. He mustered into Confederate service at Lynchburg, Virginia on 19 May 1861. His service record contains no other information.
References: Listed as C.C. Overstreet in the LMA minutes (1888), pages 7 (#73) and 81. Listed as Overstreet, Christenbury in the Roster of Confederate Soldiers 1861-1865, Vol. XII, page 78. National Archives Catalog ID: 586957, Roll 0050, page 2, Publication number M317.

Owen, J.T. (stone reads: T.J. Owens MISS)
Private, Company K, 4ᵗʰ Regiment North Carolina Infantry (State Troops)
J. T. Owen enlisted on 20 July 1863. He was a 36 years old resident of Rowan County, North Carolina when he mustered into Confederate service on 21 July 1863 at Granville County, North Carolina. On 15 September 1863, Owen was listed sick in General Hospital No. 9, Richmond, Virginia, with chronic diarrhea. He returned to duty on 2 October 1863. He was killed at Spotsylvania Court House, on 12 May 1864.
References: *Listed as J.T. Owens in the LMA minutes (1888), pages 11 (#111) and 84. Listed as Owen, J.T. in the Roster of Confederate Soldiers 1861-1865, Vol. XII, page 84. National Archives Catalog ID: 586957, Roll 0140, page 1, Publication number M 270.*

Parker, Daniel A. J. (stone reads: D. Parker ARK)
Corporal, Company F, 1ˢᵗ Regiment Arkansas Infantry
This 20 or 23 year old farmer enlisted at Little Rock, Arkansas on 8 May 1861 and mustered into Confederate service at Lynchburg, Virginia on 19 May 1861. His service record contains no other information.
References: *LMA minutes (1888), pages 3 (#15) and 83. Roster of Confederate Soldiers 1861-1865, Vol. XII, page 137. Hodge, "These We Know," page 107. National Archives Catalog ID: 586957, Roll 0050, page 2, Publication number M 317.*

Perry, Richard M. (stone reads: R.M. Perry VA)
Private, Company H, 17th Regiment Mississippi Infantry
Born in Kentucky, Richard Perry was a 30 year old married farmer living near Eureka, Mississippi when he enlisted 1 October 1862 at Panola, to serve for three years. He died of congestive chill at Fredericksburg, Virginia on 1 January 1863.
References: *LMA minutes (1888), pages 9 (#134) and 85. Roster of Confederate Soldiers 1861-1865, Vol. XII, page 281. Hodge, "These We Know," page 109. National Archives Catalog ID: 586957, Roll 0259, page 5, Publication number M269.*

Pittman, Cannon (stone reads: Pittman NC)
Private, Company B, 2nd Regiment North Carolina Infantry (State Troops)
On 24 June 1863, Cannon Pittman enlisted at Raleigh, North Carolina for the duration of the war. His service record shows that he was sick and hospitalized on or around 28 June 1863 in Wilson County. Pittman mustered into Confederate service at Wilson County North Carolina on 24 January 1864. He was killed at Spotsylvania Court House on 12 May 1864.
References: *Listed as Pittman in the LMA minutes (1888), pages 5 (#36) and 82. Listed as Pittman, Cannon in the Roster of Confederate Soldiers 1861-1865, Vol. XII, page 366. National Archives Catalog ID: 586957, Roll 0112, page 4, Publication number M270.*

Pitts, Richard C. (stone reads: Richd C. Pitts VA)
Private, Company H, 47th Regiment Virginia Infantry
Richard Pitts, of King George County, enlisted on 20 March 1862 at Fredericksburg, Virginia, for three years and/or the duration of the war. He was recorded absent without leave on 31 December 1862.
References: *Listed as Richd C. Pitts in the LMA minutes (1888), pages 5 (#44), 6, and 82. Listed as Pitts, Richard in the Roster of Confederate Soldiers 1861-1865, Vol. XII, page 371. National Archives Catalog ID: 586957, Roll 0909, page 4 Publication number M324.*

Placie, John M. (stone reads: Jno. M. Placer ARK)
Private, Company D, 1st Regiment Arkansas Infantry
This 20 year old farmer enlisted at Pine Bluff, Arkansas on 1 May 1861 to serve for one year. He mustered into Confederate service at Lynchburg,

Virginia on 19 May 1861 and died of pneumonia at a Fredericksburg hospital on 26 June 1861.

References: *Recorded as Jno. M. Placer in the LMA minutes (1888), pages 7 (#91) and 81. Recorded as Placie, John M. in the Roster of Confederate Soldiers 1861-1865 Vol. XII page 372. Hodge, "These We Know," page 110. National Archives Catalog ID: 586957, Roll 0047, page 4, Publication number M317.*

Pope, James A. (stone reads: J.A. Pope NC)
Private, Company H, 2nd Regiment North Carolina Infantry (State Troops)
A native of Wayne County, North Carolina, James Pope was 21 years old when he enlisted on 27 May 1861, to serve for the duration of the war. He died in a Fredericksburg, Virginia hospital on 24 August 1861.

References: *LMA minutes (1888), pages 3 (#34) and 82. Roster of Confederate Soldiers 1861-1865, Vol. XII, page 406. Hodge, "These We Know," page 111. North Carolina Roster, Vol. 3, page 458. National Archives Catalog ID: 586957, Roll 0112, page 3, Publication number M270.*

Pope, John B. (new stone reads: J.B. Pope VA)
Private, Company E, 40th Regiment Virginia Infantry
John Pope, of Richmond County, Virginia enlisted at Warsaw, Virginia on 4 June 1861 for one year. He mustered into Confederate service the same day. He died in Fredericksburg of unknown causes. There is a record of payment on 20 August 1861 for the burial of Pope in the amount of $15, made to William H. Norton for burial of Soldiers at Hospital No 1, Fredericksburg Virginia.

References: *LMA minutes (1888), pages 5 (#48) and 82. Roster of Confederate Soldiers 1861-1865, Vol. XII, page 406. National Archives Catalog ID: 586957, Roll 0857, page 3, Publication number M324.*

A stone marker was placed at Pope's grave site on 29 March 2008 by the Matthew Fontaine Maury Camp 1722.

Pridgers, Samuel (stone reads: Pridgan NC)
Private, Company B, 2nd Regiment North Carolina Infantry (State Troops)
Samuel Pridgers was a 21 year old resident of Wilson County, North Carolina when he enlisted on 27 May 1861. He mustered into Confederate service the same day. Pridgen died in Fredericksburg, Virginia, of unknown causes, on 8 August 1861.

References: *Recorded as Pridgan in the LMA minutes (1888), pages 5 (#54) and 82. Listed as Pridgers, Samuel in the Roster of Confederate Soldiers 1861-1865, Vol. XII, page 485. National Archives Catalog ID: 586957, Roll 0112, page 6, Publication number M270.*

Riffe, Joshua (stone reads: Jos. Rife ARK)
Private, Company B, 1st Regiment Arkansas Infantry
Joshua Riffe was an 18 year old farmer when he enlisted at Little Rock, Arkansas on 8 May 1861 and mustered into Confederate service in Lynchburg, Virginia on 19 May 1861. He died of sickness in a Fredericksburg hospital.
References: *Recorded as Joshua Rife in the LMA minutes (1888), pages 7 (#71) and 81. Listed as Riffe, Joshua in the Roster of Confederate Soldiers 1861-1865, Vol. XIII, page 168. Hodge, "These We Know," page 117. National Archives Catalog ID: 586957, Roll 0051, page 3, Publication number M317.*

Roach, William H. (stone reads: Wm. H. Roach ARK)
Private, Company H, 1st Regiment Arkansas Infantry
This 19 year old farmer enlisted at Little Rock, Arkansas on 8 May 1861 and mustered into Confederate service at Lynchburg, Virginia on 19 May 1861. His service record contains no other information.
References: *LMA minutes (1888), pages 7 (#84) and 81. Roster of Confederate Soldiers 1861-1865, Vol. XIII, page 197. Hodge, "These We Know," page 117. National Archives Catalog ID: 586957, Roll 0051, page 3, Publication number M317.*

Robinson, Samuel C. (stone reads: Saml Robinson TENN)
Private, Company D, 2nd Regiment Tennessee Infantry
Robinson was a 23 year old man from Bedford County, Tennessee when enlisted in May of 1861. He mustered into Confederate service on 17 May 1861, at Lynchburg, Virginia. There is no other information given. Robinson's service records do not show how or where he died, but he is buried in the Fredericksburg City Cemetery.
References: *Listed as Saml Robinson in the LMA minutes (1888), pages 7 (#75) and 81. Listed as Robinson, Samuel in the Roster of Confederate Soldiers 1861-1865, Vol. XIII, page 259. National Archives Catalog ID: 586957, Roll 0117, page 1, Publication number M268.*

Rogers, J. Stewart (stone reads: J.S. Rogers MISS)
Private, Company K, 13th Regiment Mississippi Infantry
Born in Alabama, this 30 year old mechanic was living near Stonewall, Mississippi when he traveled 190 miles from Marion to Corinth to enlist on 14 May 1861, to serve for one year. He died of typhoid fever at Fredericksburg, Virginia on 12 May 1863.
References: *LMA minutes (1888), pages 11 (#186) and 86. Roster of Confederate Soldiers 1861-1865, Vol. XIII, page 293. Hodge, "These We Know," page 119. National Archives Catalog ID: 586957, Roll 0218, page 14, Publication number M269.*

Sasser, Larkin P. (new stone reads: T. Sager NC)
Private, Company H, 2nd Regiment North Carolina Troops
There is no record of a T. Sarger except in the 1888 LMA minutes, where he is recorded as a Corporal in Company H. There is, however, a record of payment made to William H. Norton on 4 December 1861 for the burial of a Larkin Sasser, who died on 4 August 1861 at Camp Holmes, Stafford County, Virginia. Sasser's service records show that he enlisted at the age of 22, in May 1861, at Wayne County, North Carolina.
References: *Listed as T. Sarger in the LMA minutes (1888), pages 5 (#58) and 82. Listed as Sasser, Larkin P. in the Roster of Confederate Soldiers 1861-1865, Vol. XIII, page 444. National Archives Catalog ID: 586957, Roll 0113, pages 6, 11 Publication number M270.*

A memorial marker was placed at Sager's (Minutes spelling) grave site on 29 March 2008 by the Matthew Fontaine Maury Camp 1722.

Saunders, Harrison S. (stone reads: C.S. Samuel GA)
Private, Company D, 24th Regiment Georgia Infantry
According to the LMA minutes, C.S. Samuel was a soldier who served in Co. H of the 24th Georgia Infantry. The unit roster, however, does not include anyone in the 24th Georgia Infantry by that name. A likely match for this soldier is Harrison S. Saunders who served as a Sergeant in Company D. Saunders's service records show that he died on 10 June 1862, place not stated. The 24th Georgia Infantry was in and or around Fredericksburg between 21 May and 21 July 1862, placing Saunders near Fredericksburg, where he is buried.
References: *Listed as C.S. Samuel in the LMA minutes (1888), pages 7*

(#99) and 84. National Archives Catalog ID: 586957, Roll 0359, pages 3-5, Publication number M266.

Sawyer, William J. (stone reads: W.J. Sawyer NC)
Private, Company I, 3rd Regiment North Carolina Infantry (State Troops)
William Sawyer was born in Beaufort County, North Carolina. He enlisted on 19 June 1861 at the age of 19, to serve for the duration of the war. He died in Hospital No. 1 at Fredericksburg, Virginia on 25 August 1861.
References: *LMA minutes (1888), pages 5 (#43) and 82. Roster of Confederate Soldiers 1861-1865, Vol. XIII, page 463. National Archives Catalog ID: 586957, Roll 0131, page 1, Publication number M270.*

Scott, Benjamin F. (stone reads: Benj. Scott ARK)
Private, Company E, 1st Regiment Arkansas Infantry
On 20 February 1862, Benjamin Scott enlisted at Benton, Arkansas, to serve for two years. His service records show that he was wounded on 19-20 September 1863, at Chickamauga, Georgia, and died of his wounds on 10 October 1863, at Fredericksburg, Virginia. Within his records is a claim filed for his effects, on 12 June 1863, by Amanda B. Scott, his widow.
References: *LMA minutes (1888), pages 5 (#64) and 82. Roster of Confederate Soldiers 1861-1865, Vol. XII, page 493. National Archives Catalog ID: 586957, Roll 0051, page 7, Publication number M317.*

Shackleford, James W. (stone reads: J.W. Shackleford MISS)
Private, Company I, 18th Regiment Mississippi Infantry
James Shackleford was a 26 year old student from Camden Mississippi when he enlisted on 16 August 1861 at Leesburg or Lee's Mills, Virginia. He re-enlisted on 15 February 1862, to serve for two more years, for which he was paid a $50 bounty and granted a furlough. He was **killed in batt**le at Marye's Hill at Fredericksburg, on 3 May 1863.
References: *LMA minutes (1888), pages 9 (#140) and 85.* **Roster of** *Confederate Soldiers 1861-1865, Vol. XIV, page 3. Hodge, "These We Know," page 123. National Archives Catalog ID: 586957, Roll 0273,* **page 11,** *Publication number M269.*

Shepherd, Gordon (stone reads: Gordon Shepherd VA)
Private, Company A, 30th Regiment Virginia Infantry
On 22 April 1861, at the age of 22, Gordon Shepherd enlisted at Fredericksburg, Virginia. His service records show that he was absent sick at home and later discharged from service on 3 May 1862.
References: *LMA minutes (1888), page 85. National Archives Catalog ID: 586957, Roll 0768, page 2, Publication number M324.*

Smith, John H. (stone reads: J.H. Smith MISS)
Sergeant, Company I, 18th Regiment Mississippi Volunteers
This 19 or 23 year old student from Brownsville, Mississippi traveled 245 miles to enlist at Corinth, to serve for one year. He was promoted to Corporal on 1 February 1862 and to Sergeant on 25 April 1862. He re-enlisted at Lee's Mills, Virginia on 26 April 1862, to serve for two more years. He was killed in battle at Marye's Hill, at Fredericksburg, on 3 May 1863.
References: *LMA minutes (1888), pages 11 (#180) and 85. Roster of Confederate Soldiers 1861-1865, Vol. XIV, page 251. Hodge, "These We Know," page 127. National Archives Catalog ID: 586957, Roll 0274, page 14, Publication number M269.*

Sneed, Alex (stone reads: Alex. Snead MISS)
Corporal, Virginia Light Artillery
The LMA minutes state that Alex Sneed was from Mississippi, but in April 1862 he enlisted in Richmond, Virginia, at the age of 27. He was sworn into Confederate service by Captain J. W. Lewis on 8 April 1862, for three years or the duration of war. He was promoted on 24 July 1862 from Private to Corporal. On 17 November 1862, Sneed was reported killed in action. Advance elements of the Union army arrived at Fredericksburg that day and Sneed's light artillery battery fired on the arriving Federals. A New York battery responded with very accurate fire and scattered the Confederate guns. Sneed was one of the casualties.
References: *Listed as Alex. Snead in the LMA minutes (1888), pages 9 (#112) and 84. Listed as Sneed, Alex D. in the Roster of Confederate Soldiers 1861-1865, Vol., XIV page 315. National Archives Catalog ID: 586957, Roll 0093, page 6, Publication number M329.*

Southerland, William J. (new stone reads: James Southard)
Private, Company C, 12th Regiment North Carolina Troops (formerly 2nd North Carolina Infantry, Volunteers)
On 22 April 1861, a 20 year old William Southerland enlisted at Kenansville, North Carolina. On 18 May 1861, he mustered into Confederate service, for 6 months, at Raleigh North Carolina. His service record shows him named on a "Roll of Honor," date not stated. The LMA register names this man as James Southard and notes a small wooden stake at his grave site. On page 18, however, his name is spelled "Southerland" and listed as killed on 26 December 1861.
References: *Listed as James Southard in the LMA minutes (1888), pages 18 and 85. Roster of Confederate Soldiers 1861-1865 Vol. XIV, page 341. National Archives Catalog ID: 586957, Roll 0209, page 6, Publication number M307.*
    The Matthew Fontaine Maury Camp 1722 of the Sons of Confederate Veterans placed a new marker on 29 March 2008

Stephens, Eli E. (stone reads: E.E. Stephens MISS)
Sergeant, Company A, 17th Regiment Mississippi Infantry
This soldier's service records were intermixed with Eli E. Stephens of Buena Vista, Company A, 17th Mississippi. This Sergeant Stephens, however, was 30 years old when he traveled 95 miles to enlist at Corinth, Mississippi on 30 May 1861, to serve for one year. He was promoted to Sergeant on 25 July 1862 and received mortal wounds on 29 May 1863 near Fredericksburg, Virginia (Chancellorsville campaign).
References: *LMA minutes (1888), pages 7 (#104) and 83. Roster of Confederate Soldiers 1861-1865, Vol. XIV, page 442. Hodge, "These We Know," page 131. National Archives Catalog ID: 586957, Roll 0260, pages 14-15, Publication number M269.*

Stevens, Samuel H. (stone reads: Sam. Stevens ARK)
Private, Company C, 18th Regiment North Carolina Infantry (State Troops)
Samuel Stevens, from Arkansas, enlisted on 21 April 1861 in Whiteville, North Carolina. He was 5 feet 9 ½ inches tall, 26 years old, and had walked 90 miles to muster into Confederate service on 1 May 1861. He was killed at Fredericksburg on 13 December 1862. Within the same unit was a Samuel Stephens, who was also shot at Fredericksburg and taken to Richmond for care. That Stephens died on 23 April 1863.

References: Listed as Sam Stevens in the *LMA minutes (1888)*, pages 3 (#6) and 83. Listed as Stevens, Samuel H. in the *Roster of Confederate Soldiers 1861-1865*, Vol. XIV, page 462. National Archives Catalog ID: 586957, Roll 0049, page 10, Publication number M 267.

Stewart, Lacy (stone reads: Lacy Stewart K 24 GA)
1st Lieutenant, Company K, 24th Regiment Georgia Infantry
Stewart enlisted on 20 August 1861, probably in Habersham County, Georgia. He was mustered into State service on 29 August 1861 and into Confederate service on 7 September 1861. Lieutenant Stewart was killed at Chancellorsville on 3 May 1863. Both the LMA minutes and the Roster of Confederate Soldiers spell his name as Stewart. The headstone reads Steward.
References: Listed as Lacy Stewart in the *LMA minutes (1888)*, pages 9 (#149) and 85. *Roster of Confederate Soldiers 1861-1865*, Vol. XIV, page 478. *Georgia Roster*, Vol. 3, page 80. Hodge, "These We Know," page 130. National Archives Catalog ID: 586957, Roll 0360, page 4, 5 Publication number M266.

Stidham, Jobus M. (stone reads: Jas. M. Stedham ARK)
Private, Company I, 1st Regiment Arkansas Infantry
Jobus Stidham, a farmer, was born in 1838. On 8 May 1861, at the age of 23, he enlisted at Monticello, Arkansas. On 3 August 1861, he died of disease at Fredericksburg, Virginia.
References: Listed as Jas. M. Stedham in the *LMA minutes (1888)*, pages 5 (#61) and 82. In his Compiled Service Record, his name is spelled Stidham. Listed as Stidham, Jobus M. in the *Roster of Confederate Soldiers 1861-1865*, Vol. XIV, page 485. National Archives Catalog ID: 586957, Roll 0051, page 4, Publication number M317.

Stott, Addison D. (stone reads: Addison D. Stott NC)
Private, Company B, 2nd Regiment North Carolina Infantry (State Troops)
Stott was 22 years old and lived in Wilson County, North Carolina when he enlisted on 28 May 1861, to serve for the duration of the war. He died in camp of typhoid fever, in Stafford County, Virginia, on 4 August 1861.
References: *LMA minutes (1888)*, pages 5 (#57) and 82. *Roster of Confederate Soldiers 1861-1865*, Vol. XIV, page 517. *North Carolina Roster*, Vol. 3, page 398. Hodge, "These We Know," page 132. National Archives Catalog ID: 586957, Roll 0113, page 3, Publication number M270.

Stowers, Lawrence P. (stone reads: Lawrence Stamess NC)
Private, Company E, 1ˢᵗ Regiment Arkansas Infantry
Stamess Lawrence is not found in any North Carolina roster. A likely match for this soldier is Stowers, Lawrence P., who enlisted on 26 August 1861 and died in Fredericksburg, Virginia on 24 September 1861. Charles Stowers, his father, filed a death claim on 2 July 1863, in the amount of $36 for pay due him from 26 April 1861.
References: *Listed as Lawrence Stamess in the LMA minutes (1888), pages 3 (#9) and 83. Listed as Stowers, Lawrence P. in the Roster of Confederate Soldiers 1861-1865, Vol. XIV, page 524. National Archives Catalog ID: 586957, Roll 0051, page 2, Publication number M 317.*

Sutton, William (stone reads: W. Sutton NC)
Private, Company H, 2ⁿᵈ Regiment North Carolina Infantry (State Troops)
Born and residing in Duplin County, North Carolina, William Sutton was 22 years old when he enlisted in Wayne County, on 27 May 1861, to serve for the duration of the war. He died in a hospital in Fredericksburg, Virginia on 4 September 1861.
References: *LMA minutes (1888), pages 3 (#29) and 83. Roster of Confederate Soldiers 1861-1865, Vol. XV, page 34. North Carolina Roster, Vol. III, page 459. Hodge, "These We Know," page 133. National Archives Catalog ID: 586957, Roll 0113, page 5, Publication number M270.*

Taylor, James (stone reads: Jas. Taylor NC)
Private, Company A, 2ⁿᵈ Regiment North Carolina Infantry (State Troops)
Taylor enlisted on 2 June 1861 at Fort Caswell, Wilmington, North Carolina, to serve for the duration of the war. He died on 10 August 1861 at Camp Holmes, Stafford County, Virginia.
References: *LMA minutes (1888), pages 5 (#49) and 82. Roster of Confederate Soldiers 1861-1865, Vol. XV, page 106. Hodge, "These We Know," page 135. National Archives Catalog ID: 586957, Roll 0113, page 2, Publication number M270.*

Tilley, Edmund (stone reads: Edmd Tilly NC)
Private, Company H, 22ⁿᵈ Regiment North Carolina Infantry
Edmund Tilley enlisted on 1 June 1861, at the age of 21 in Stokes County, North Carolina. He agreed to serve for one year and received a bounty payment of $10. On 25 August 1861, he was reported sick in Fredericksburg Virginia and died of disease there 5 September 1861.

References: LMA minutes (1888), pages 3 (#28) and 83. *Roster of Confederate Soldiers 1861-1865,* Vol. XV, page 259. Hodge, "These We Know," page 137. National Archives Catalog ID: 586957, Roll 0292, page 2, Publication number M270.

Trott, Newton (stone reads: Norton Trots NC)
Private, Company G, 3rd Regiment North Carolina Infantry (State Troops)
This 18 year old resident of Onslow County, North Carolina enlisted on 1 July 1861, to serve for the duration of the war. He died 1 September 1861 in a hospital at Fredericksburg, Virginia.
References: Listed as Norton Trots in the LMA minutes (1888), pages 5 (#38) and 82. Listed as Trott, Newton in the *Roster of Confederate Soldiers 1861-1865,* Vol. XIV, page 331. Hodge, "These We Know," page 138. National Archives Catalog ID: 586957, Roll 0133, page 3, Publication number M270.

Trussle Joseph A. John (stone reads: J.A.J. Trusell MISS)
Private, Company C, 13th Regiment Mississippi Infantry
Born near Big Oak, Mississippi, this 22 year old farmer, with fair complexion, light hair and dark eyes, enlisted on 14 May 1861 at Corinth, Mississippi. He was absent sick on 15 October 1862 and returned to duty on 31 October 1862. He was mortally wounded at Fredericksburg, during the Chancellorsville campaign, and died on 6 May 1863.
References: Listed as J.A.J. Trussell in the LMA minutes (1888), pages 11 (#173) and 84. Noted as Trussle, J.A.J. in the *Roster of Confederate Soldiers 1861-1865,* Vol. XV, page 339. National Archives Catalog ID: 586957, Roll 0219, page 12, Publication number M 269.

Tubbs, Samuel (stone: Sam Tubbs ARK)
Private, Company E, 1st Regiment Arkansas Infantry
This 24 year old farmer from Benton, Arkansas enlisted at Little Rock, Arkansas on 8 May 1861, to serve for one year. He mustered into Confederate service at Lynchburg, Virginia on 19 May 1861. He died 21 June 1861 at or near Fredericksburg.
References: Listed as Sam Tubbs in the LMA minutes (1888), pages 7 (#87) and 81. Listed as Tubbs, Samuel in the *Roster of Confederate Soldiers 1861-1865,* Vol. XV, page 340. Hodge, "These We Know," page 139. National Archives Catalog ID: 586957, Roll 0052, page 3, Publication number M317.

Unknown
There are 27 soldiers listed as unknown on the LMA roster. There are also additional blank stones that were not noted on the 1888 list. There could also be others that were unmarked.

Vaughan, Carter (stone reads: Vaughan Carter VA)
Laborer, 1ˢᵗ (Stonewall) Brigade
There is no one named Vaughan Carter in any Virginia unit roster. There is, however, a Carter Vaughan, who served as a laborer. National Archives records show that Carter Vaughan was a "Free Negro," who joined the Confederate Army as a laborer at Gordonsville, Virginia, in November of 1862. No other information is provided.
References: *LMA minutes (1888), pages 3 (#30) and 83. There is neither a Carter Vaughan nor a Vaughan Carter in the Roster of Confederate Soldiers 1861-1865. National Archives Catalog ID: 586957, Roll 0403, page 1, Publication number M347.*

Walker, H. A. (stone reads: A. Walker GA)
Private, Company A, 2ⁿᵈ Regiment Georgia Infantry
On 20 June 1861, Walker enlisted at Camp Semmes, Georgia. He served for 10 months and 13 days. On 30 June 1861, he was absent in a hospital at Richmond, Virginia. According to his service record, he was later reported: "Absent. Left in Hospital, Fredericksburg, Va. Supposed to be dead. No official notice."
References: *Listed as A. Walker in the LMA minutes (1888), pages 3 (#26) and 83. Listed as Walker, H.A. In the Roster of Confederate Soldiers 1861-1865, Vol. XV, page 515. National Archives Catalog ID: 586957, Roll 0156, page 2, Publication number M270.*

Weeks, S. S. (stone reads: S.S. Wicks MISS)
Private, Companies D and I, 13ᵗʰ Regiment Mississippi Infantry
Weeks traveled 200 miles to enlist at Corinth, Mississippi on 13 May 1861. He was 18 years old and agreed to serve for one year. He received a $50 bounty when he reenlisted. He was killed in battle at Fredericksburg on 4 May 1863 (Chancellorsville campaign).
References: *Listed as S.S. Wicks in the LMA minutes (1888), pages 9 (#143) and 85. Listed as Weeks, S.S. In the Roster of Confederate Soldiers 1861-1865,*

Vol. XVI, page 90. Hodge, "These We Know," page 145. National Archives Catalog ID: 586957, Roll 0200, page 13, Publication number M269.

White, Albert W. (stone missing)
Private, Company K, 13th Regiment Mississippi Infantry
At the age of 19, Albert White traveled 190 miles to enlist on 14 May 1861. White was a farmer and agreed to serve for one year. On 31 December 1861, he was promoted from Private to Corporal. On 3 May 1863, he was mortally wounded at Chancellorsville and died in Fredericksburg, Virginia on 25 May 1863.
References: *Listed as A.W. White in the LMA minutes (1888), pages 7 (#98) and 83. Listed as White, Albert W. in the Roster of Confederate soldiers 1861-1865, Vol. XVI, page 165. National Archives Catalog ID: 586957, Roll 0220, page 13, Publication number M 269.*

Wilder, Reuben L. W. (stone reads: L.W. Wilder ARK)
Private, Company B, 1st Regiment Arkansas Infantry
Reuben Wilder was a 21 year old school teacher when he enlisted at Little Rock or Arkadelphia, Arkansas, on 8 May 1861, to serve for one year. He was reported sick in a hospital in Fredericksburg, Virginia and died there on 12 July 1861.
References: *Listed as L.W. Wilder in the LMA minutes (1888), pages 7 (#79) and 81. Listed as Wilder, Reuben in the Roster of Confederate Soldiers 1861-1865, Vol. XVI, page 244. Hodge, "These We Know," page 148. National Archives Catalog ID: 586957, Roll 0052, pages 3-4, Publication number M317.*

Williams, Joseph G. (stone reads: J.G. Williams ARK)
Private, Company D, 1st Regiment Arkansas Infantry
This 19 year old farmer enlisted at Pine Bluff, Arkansas on 1 May 1861 and mustered into Confederate service at Lynchburg Virginia on 19 May 1861. He died at Fredericksburg, Virginia.
References: *LMA minutes (1888), pages 3 (#12) and 83. Roster of Confederate Soldiers 1861-1865, Vol. XVI, page 309. Hodge, "These We Know," page 149. National Archives Catalog ID: 586957, Roll 0015, page 1, Publication number M 372.*

Williams, George W. (stone reads: Geo. Williams NC)
Private, Company E, 1st Regiment North Carolina Troops
This 18 year old man enlisted on 20 June 1861, at Wilmington, North Carolina, to serve for the duration of the war. He died of disease, but no place or date is given.
References: *Listed as Geo. Williams in the LMA minutes (1888), pages 9 (#128) and 85. Listed as Williams, George W. in the Roster of Confederate Soldiers 1861-1865, Vol. XVI, page 287. Hodge, "These We Know," page 149. National Archives Catalog ID: 586957, Roll 0099, page 3, Publication number M 270.*

Wills, I. B. (stone reads: W.G. Willig Segt LA)
Sergeant, Company A, 9th Regiment Louisiana Infantry
There is no one named Willig in any Louisiana regimental roster. A likely match for this soldier is I.B. Wills. His service records shows that he was taken a prisoner and paroled at Warrenton, Virginia on 29 September 1862 with no further details given. Sergeant Wills is buried next to Captain Cummings who fought with the 9th Louisiana Infantry and was killed 4 May 1863 at Smith Run, Fredericksburg Virginia, during the Chancellorsville campaign.
References: *Listed as W.G. Willig in the LMA minutes (1888), pages 7 (#97) and 83. Listed as Wills, I.B. in the Roster of Confederate Soldiers 1861-1865, Vol. XVI, page 361. National Archives Catalog ID: 586957, Roll 0214, page 1, Publication number M 320.*

Witherspoon John G. (stone reads: Jno. Witherspoon MISS)
Private, Company E, 48th Regiment Mississippi Volunteers
  On 17 September 1863, Witherspoon enlisted at Enterprise, Mississippi, to serve for the duration of the war. His service record shows that on 11 November 1863 he was in the General Hospital at Howard Grove, in Richmond, suffering from pleurisy. On 23 November 1863, Witherspoon is recorded as having deserted from the Richmond Hospital. His records do not show how he died, yet his remains are buried along the west wall of the City Cemetery in Fredericksburg, Virginia.
References: *Witherspoon, John G. is listed in the Roster of Confederate Soldiers 1861-1865, Vol. XVI, page 436, but not in the LMA Minute Book of 1888. National Archives Catalog ID: 586957, Roll 0422, page 14, Publication number M 269.*

Woodard, John D. (stone reads: J.D. Woodward MISS)
Private, Company C, 48th Regiment Mississippi Volunteers
John Woodard enlisted on 19 July 1861 in Mississippi, place not stated, and was mustered into Confederate service by a Major Gregory, for the duration of the war. He was wounded in battle at Sharpsburg, on 17 September 1862. His service record shows that he died on 3 June 1864 from wounds received on 12 May 1864, place not stated, but presumably Spotsylvania Court House.
References: *In the LMA minutes (1888), pages 9 (#147) and 85, Woodard is recorded as a private, serving in Company D, 18th Mississippi Infantry. Other records, however, show him in Company C, 48th Mississippi Infantry. He is listed as Woodard, John D., of the 48th Mississippi Regiment in the Roster of Confederate Soldiers 1861-1865, Vol. XVI, page 469. National Archives Catalog ID: 586957, Roll 0422, page 18, Publication number M269.*

Wootan Thomas J. (stone reads: Jos. T.J. Wroten MISS)
Private, Companies F and C, 13th Regiment Mississippi Infantry
On 14 May 1861, Thomas Wootan, a 22 year old farmer from Big Oaks, Mississippi enlisted at Corinth, Mississippi for one year. He was 5 feet 11 inches tall, dark in complexion, with dark hair and dark eyes. His service records show that "he was mortally wounded at Fredericksburg Virginia 3 May 1863 and died 6 May 1863."
References: *Listed as Jos. T.J. Wroten in the LMA minutes (1888), pages 11 (#174) and 84. Listed as Wootan, Thomas J. in the Roster of Confederate Soldiers 1861-1865, Vol. XVI, page 495. National Archives Catalog ID: 586957, Roll 0220, pages 5 and 14, Publication number M269.*

Young, Nathan M. (stone reads: Nathan Young ARK)
Corporal, Company E, 1st Regiment Arkansas Infantry
This 23 year old farmer enlisted on 26 April 1861 at Benton, Arkansas and mustered into Confederate service at Lynchburg, Virginia on 19 May 1861. He was sick in a hospital at Fredericksburg, Virginia, where he died.
References: *LMA minutes (1888) pages 7 (#74) and 81. Roster of Confederate Soldiers 1861-1865, Vol. XVI, page 581. Hodge, "These We Know," page 153. National Archives Catalog ID: 586957, Roll 0052, page 3, Publication number M317.*

THE WEST WALL SOLDIERS

Shall
I read
The names
Once claimed
Of
Those so dearer than life?
And feel the grief of those
So near
Whose hearts were broken,
Stricken,
By the blow of a single name
As
Life was shattered,
And weary hope lost.
Lamented cries
Heard long, and aloud,
my James!
my John!
my Thomas!
A Mother's whisper,
Speaks solemn words
"He was my pretty boy… who I sang to sleep
So many times in my arms"
In anguish,
Torn,
She folds in grief
Uttering Moans,
Sounds,
Of Inexpressible description
Alas!
For the hearts that feel!
Alas!
For the eyes that read!
Of broken limbs in hospital halls
Or ghastly faces which lie cold white on battlefield grounds
Shall I read?
Oh
Shall I read?
As
The terrible blow falls on our homes throughout the land?

By Roy B. Perry, Jr.

At war's end, the occupying Union force established its headquarters in the National Bank, then called the Farmer's Bank, at the corner of Princess Anne and George Streets. Colonel E.V. Sumner, commanding the garrison, reached his office through the George Street entry, on the left. Anyone seeking the Adjutant General or the Provost Marshal used the Princess Anne Street entry on the right. (Fredericksburg Ledger, June 10, 1865).

Minutes of the Common Council of the Town of Fredericksburg, 1864-1865

TRANSCRIBED AND ANNOTATED BY ERIK F. NELSON

Fredericksburg's Town Council had to handle its local affairs while armies crashed through their community. Their minutes attest to routine affairs such as setting tax rates, handling drainage issues, hiring police officers, and so on, but superimposed on this familiar activity is the Civil War. The Town Council's record in 1864 and 1865 shows gaps in the meeting schedule, which often appears to have been related to martial activity. The record also shows the elected body dealing with civil/military matters, both dangerous as well as ludicrous.

In 1864, the Town Council did not meet at all in February. They may simply have had no business to conduct during a hard winter, but Confederate President Jefferson Davis was concerned enough about Southern morale to call attention to the need to overcome "discontent" and "disaffection." The month of May saw the beginning of the Overland Campaign, which brought thousands of wounded soldiers to Fredericksburg and a temporary Federal administration. An ill-advised effort to take Union stragglers prisoner resulted in a harsh response from the Union army, and the Council had to deal with a prisoner exchange, similar to what had occurred in 1862. The period from August 13 to October 5 was entirely free of meetings. During that time, Atlanta fell and a Federal army crushed Confederate forces in the Shenandoah Valley, neither of which would have had any local effect, but which certainly suggested that the Confederate experience might not end well.

In 1865, the Town Council meetings occurred on a more regular basis, but in the spring there was a six week gap between meetings. During that period, seemingly endless columns of Federal troops marched through the area. The Army of the Potomac moved north, after the surrender at Appomattox, and the western army that had marched with William T. Sherman through Georgia and the Carolinas also marched through Fredericksburg, on its way to Washington for a grand review. The Federal columns crossed on pontoon bridges set up at Franklin's crossing, just downstream of Fredericksburg and at the United States Ford, several miles upstream of the town. The sheer number of Federal soldiers that passed through the area for more than two weeks had to have been sobering.

In the 1930s, the Works Progress Administration typed out the Town Council's hand written minutes. These typescripts contain a few typing errors, which have been corrected by checking them against the original record. In addition, the first draft of some of the Council's minutes have survived and these too have been examined for any additional material left out of the record copy. Missing words and sentences lost in the recopying have been inserted here and identified by brackets. Variations in spelling and abbreviating have been left intact.

1864

At a Called Meeting of the Common Council of the Town of Fred[erick]sburg, at the Mayor's Office, on Monday January 25th, 1864–

Present–M. Slaughter, Mayor

    Wm. A. Little, Recorder

        J. Gordon Wallace, Wm. H. Cunningham, Lau. B. Rose, James McGuire, Jas. H. Bradley, J.G. Hurkamp.

An account of Dr. J.G. Wallace against the Corporation amounting to $5. is allowed and ordered to be paid.

An account of John Timberlake, late Jailor of this Corporation, [a/c] amounting to $75.75, is allowed and ordered to be paid.

On the Petition of John L. Andrews setting forth that he had lost during the occupation of a part of the County of Spotsylvania, by the Yankey Army during the Spring &[and] Summer of 1862, 24 bonds of $100 each, issued by the Corporation of Fredericksburg to Andrews & Quisenberry and of which he was the assignee, and asking that duplicates thereof be issued to him, On Consideration whereof the Council doth direct and order that the Chamberlain issue duplicates of said bonds upon the said John L. Andrews entering into bond with security, to be approved by the

Chamberlain with [in the] penalty of $4,800, Conditioned to indemnify & save harmless the Corporation from all loss damage or injury which he may sustain or be liable to sustain by reason of issuing such duplicates, & that he pay the expenses thereby incurred.[1]

On motion, Ordered that the Chamberlain issue to Wm. J. Jeffries a new bond for $100 in place of a mutilated one for that Amount, which has been delivered over to the Chamberlain.

Mr. D. H. Gordon by note in writing resigned his office as a member of this board, which resignation was on motion received.

The Council proceeded to elect a member of the board to supply the vacancy occasioned by the resignation of Mr. D.H. Gordon, when Mr. Geo. W. Eve was duly elected.

On motion, Ordered that the Chamberlain cause the Commissioners books for the year 1862 to be brought from their present place of deposit to his office in the Town of Fredericksburg, to be turned over by him to the Finance Committee.

An Account of G.F. Chew amtg. to $20. is allowed & ordered to be paid.

An account of Kelly Tackett Ford & Co. amounting to $320.25 is allowed and Ordered to be paid.

Three accounts of Wm. Henry amounting in the aggregate to the sum of $1,006.00 are [is] allowed & ordered to be paid.

The Committee heretofore appointed to invest the sum of $50,000 paid over to them by M. Slaughter, Treasurer of the Relief fund in 7 ½ ct Coupon bond of the Confederate States, made a report in writing in the word and figures following to wit: To the Mayor & Common Council of Fredg,

Gentlemen: [Fredg. Jany 25th 1864]

The undersigned respectfully report that in pursuance of the directions of the Common Council at their former meeting, they proceeded to invest the sum of $50,000 in 7 per cent Coupon bonds of the Confederate States, which they purchased at $100.50 the premium of ½ per cent on $250. being paid by a draft through John M. Herndon on Geo. F. Chew, Chamberlain of the Corporation, said bonds were deposited by Mr. Herndon in the Bank of Virginia at Richmond for safe keeping & Mr. Herndon was requested to ascertain whether said Coupon bonds can be transferred into registered bonds of the Confederate States, & to make the change if it can be done.

The amount directed to be paid over to the Chamberlain, at said Meeting of Council, of $18,000 for the [use] of the Overseers of the Poor, and of $25,000 to same for the purchase of bonds of the Corp. of Fredg. by the Finance Committee, have been duly paid over by Mr. Slaughter, Treas. of relief fund to said Chamberlain.

Respectfully submitted, M. Slaughter, J.H. Bradley, W.A. Little,

Which Report having been read was adopted & ordered to be spread in the Minutes of the proceedings.

The Mayor appointed Mr. Wm. A. Little a member of the Finance Committee in the room and stead of D.H. Gordon, resigned.

Mr. James A. Taylor resigned his office as Police Officer of this Corp. to take place on the 15th Dec. 1863, which resignation was on motion received.

On motion, the Council then Adjd.

M. Slaughter, Mayor

At a Called Meeting of the Common Council of the Town of Fredericksburg, held at the Mayor's Office on the 5th day of March 1864–

Present– M. Slaughter, Mayor
      Wm. A. Little, Recorder
      G.(sic) G. Wallace, Horace B. Hall, Wm. H. Cunningham,
      Jas.H. Bradley, [J.G. Hurkamp,] Jno. J. Young.

The following Accounts were passed and ordered to be paid:

James T. Kendall	$147.00
Geo. Gravatt	6.00
M. Slaughter	237.50

On motion of Mr. J.G. Wallace, Ordered that the Finance Committee be and they are hereby directed to cause to be deposited in the Virginia Bank at Richmond to the Credit of Jno. M. Clarkson, Supt., the sum of $4,022 to pay for 200 bushels of salt for the use of the inhabitants of this Corp.

On motion, the Council then Adjd.

M. Slaughter, Mayor

At a Meeting of the Common Council of the Town of Fredericksburg at the Court house, on Monday Morning the 21st day of M[ar]ch. 1864–
Present–Wm. A. Little, Recorder, L.B. Rose, J.G. Hurkamp, J.J. Young, H.B. Hall, Jas. McGuire.

There not being a quorum present for the dispatch of other business, the Members present ordered the polls to be opened for the election of twelve Councilmen, this being the day fixed by law for that purpose, and the Voters having cast their ballots [it was found in counting the same, that the Votes were as follows],Viz: For Wm. A. Little 160, J.G. Hurkamp 149, J.M. Herndon 129, G.W. Eve 117, B.T. Gill 116, W.H. Cunningham 112, J.W. Sener 109, H.B. Hall 103, J.H. Bradley 93, J.J. Young 93, L.B. Rose 98, J. McGuire 89, Geo. Gravatt 80, J.G. Read 67, P.P. Burr 53, Geo. Gillman 53 & C. Armat 48, the first named twelve of whom were declared duly elected.

And then [the] Council Adjourned.

Council Chamber, March 21st, 1864.
Wm. A. Little, J.G. Hurkamp, G.W. Eve, Wm.H. Cunningham, H.B. Hall, Jas.H. Bradley, J.J. Young, L.B. Rose & J. McGuire & B.T. Gill,
Members elect of the Common Council of the Town of Fred[erick]sburg met at the Council Chamber and severally took the oaths of office before J. Gordon Wallace, Esqr., a Justice for the Corporation of Fredericksburg.

On motion Jas. H. Bradley was called to the chair.

The salary of the Mayor was fixed at One thousand dollars.

The Council then proceeded to the election of a Mayor, when Montgomery Slaughter was elected and took the several oaths of office before J.G. Wallace, Esqr., a Justice of the Peace for the Corporation of Fred[erick]sburg.

Mr. Wm. A. Little was duly elected Recorder of the Corporation and took the oaths of office before J.G. Wallace, a Mayor(sic) of the Peace for the Corporation of Fred[erick]sburg.

On motion, the Salaries of the following officers were fixed as follows,
The Clerk of the Council at Two hundred dollars.
The Chamberlain of the Corporatiion at Eight hundred dollars.
The Commissioner of the Revenue at Five hundred dollars.
The Collector of Taxes and Rents, at Five per cent on the amount collected.
Geo[rge] F. Chew was elected Clerk of the Council & Chamberlain.

Rob[er]t. W. Hart, Commissioner of the Revenue.

L.J. Huffman, Collector of Taxes & Rents

Surveyor–

Inspector & Measurer of Lumber, Wood &c

Weigher & Measurer of coal, grain, salt &c.

On motion, the number of Police Officers for the Current Year was fixed at two and their Salaries were fixed at Five hundred dollars each per annum.

The Council then proceeded to elect Police officers for the Current Year, when James T. Kendall and James A. Taylor were elected on the first ballot.

The Tax on Drays, Carts & Wagons for the present year was fixed as follows, Viz: On Drays & Carts $15-, And on Wagons $30.-

The Mayor appointed the following standing Committees for the year, Viz:

On Finance–John M. Herndon, Wm. A. Little, J.H. Bradley.

On Public Property–Wm. H. Cunningham, J.G. Hurkamp, & James McGuire.

On Streets–J.J. Young, Geo. W. Eve, B.T. Gill

On Pumps–J.W. Sener, H.B. Hall, L.B. Rose

On motion, Ordered that the Public Property Committee be & they are hereby instructed to enquire & ascertain what price can be obtained for the Fire Engines & apparatus & whether it is desirable to dispose of the same and report the result of their deliberating to the Council.

On motion, Ordered that the Public Property Committee be & they are hereby instructed to have the roof of the Court house & other buildings repaired if deemed necessary & practicable.

On motion, ordered that James H. Bradley, J.J Young & John G. Hurkamp be and they are hereby authorized to purchase from two [to] five hundred bushels of corn & other [grain] for distribution among the needy Citizens of the Town at costs & charges.

Rob[er]t W. Hart, James T. Kendall, James A. Taylor severally took the oaths of office before the Mayor.

On motion, the Council than Adjd.

M. Slaughter, Mayor

At a Called Meeting of the Common Council of the Town of Fred[erick]sburg, held at the Mayor's office on the 14th day of April 1864–
Present–William A. Little, Recorder
John J. Young, John G. Hurkamp, Geo. W. Eve, Joseph W. Sener, James H. Bradley, B[everley]T. Gill,
Common Councilmen–

The Recorder stated that the Council had been convened for the purpose of cooperating with the Corporation Court in an application to the Secretary of the Treasury to be relieved from Confederate taxation for the present, whereupon on motion the Council unanimously adopted the proceedings of the court & concurred in the appointment of M. Slaughter, Mayor & T.B. Barton, atty. for the Comnwth. as a committee to present said application.

Joseph W. Sener appeared, was qualified and took his seat at the board. The following persons were appointed overseers of the poor [for the] Town, to serve until the next annual appointment, Viz: James H. Bradley, Charles B. Waite, John G. Hurkamp, Jno. L. Knight, James McGuire and L.J. Huffman.

An account of E. Stephens for burying an infant child found dead, amounting to ten dollars was presented and ordered to be paid.

On motion the Council adj[ourne]d

Wm. A. Little, Recorder

At a Meeting of the Common Council of the Town of Fred[erick]sburg, at the Mayor's office on the 30th day of April 1864–
Present–M. Slaughter, Mayor
Wm. A. Little, Recorder, J.G. Hurkamp, L.B. Rose, Jas. McGuire, J.W. Sener, J.J. Young, B.T. Gill & James H. Bradley.

On motion of Mr. Jas. H. Bradley, Messrs. Wm. A. Little, Jas. H. Bradley & John F. Scott were appointed a Committee to confer with the assessor as to the Assessed value of Real Estate in the Town of Fredg. for taxation by the Confederate States Government and to report to the Council.

On motion, Ordered that the Agent for the delivery of salt do furnish each individual entitled thereto with 25 lbs. of salt at 13 cents per pound in new issue.

Ordered that the account of Slaughter &c for expenses of freight on the

Corp. Salt amounting to $2919.35 be paid by the Chamberlain and that the Mayor tender to the said firm the thanks of the Council for their kindness in attending to the business without charge.

On motion, the Council then Adjd.

M. Slaughter, [Mayor]

At a Called Meeting of the Common Council of the Town of Fredericksburg, at the Mayor's office on the 3rd day of May 1864 –

Present–M. Slaughter, Mayor, Wm. A. Little, Recorder,
J.G. Hurkamp, H.B. Hall, James McGuire,
G. W. Eve, B.T. Gill, J.J. Young.

Mr. Wm. A. Little, Chairman of the Committee appointed at the last meeting of the Council to confer with the Assessor as to the value to be assessed on the real Estate in the Town of Fred[erick]sburg for Taxation by the Confederate States Government, made a report in writing, which report having been read, it was adopted and ordered to be filed and a Copy thereof furnished to the Assessor.

The following Resolution was unanimously adopted, Viz: Resolved, That the Commissary General be respectfully requested to abstain from impressing articles of food meat &c in the Town of Fredericksburg when in fact there is but very little food of any sort, and the population are actually in danger of starvation, and when we believe that the supply of meat at present instead of being sufficient to permit us to have ½ a supply for the people for six months would not in fact furnish a ½ supply for the people for 1 month. And we Respectfully suggest that the meat recently impressed by Capt. Roy in the store of Mess. Heinichen & Berry & Co. & which was perhaps the only meat in any quantity for sale in the Town be released from said impressment.

On Motion, the Council Adjd.

M. Slaughter, Mayor

Editor's Note:
On May 5, the 1864 Overland Campaign opened with a battle in the Wilderness, on the western edge of Spotsylvania County. Within a few days, the fighting had moved south, to Spotsylvania Court House. Battles knock loose soldiers from their commands and some of the walking wounded as well as many

stragglers followed the Plank Road out of the Wilderness to Fredericksburg. According to local citizen Edward L. Heinichen, they quietly sought a way across the Rappahannock River at the Falmouth Ford. On May 8, however, Town Councilmember John F. Scott, over the protests of other Councilmembers, took it upon himself to gather a group of citizens together and place a number of these stragglers under arrest, forwarding them to Confederate authorities as prisoners. Fredericksburg would become a vast hospital during this period and arriving Federal authorities were not amused with civilians interjecting themselves into military affairs. On May 20, they responded by taking into custody a corresponding number of local citizens who would subsequently be exchanged for the arrested soldiers. Heinichen described John Scott's actions as "foolish." A similar situation had developed in the spring of 1862, when local authorities thought it a good idea to arrest local citizens who remained loyal to the Union and send them to Richmond as prisoners. The Federal army that occupied the town in April 1862 arrested a corresponding number of citizens, who were subsequently exchanged for the loyalist citizens.[2]

At a Called Meeting of the Common Council of the Town of Fred[erick]sburg, held on the 31st day of May 1864 –
Present–M. Slaughter, Mayor, Wm. A. Little, Recorder
        Wm. H. Cunningham, H.B. Hall, J.J. Young, L.B. Rose, J.G. Hurkamp, James McGuire, [Jas. H. Bradley],
        Common Councilmen.

The Mayor stated that the Council had been called for the purpose of taking steps for the relief of our Citizens who have been arrested as hostages by the Enemy, and who are now confined at Fort Delaware, And thereupon, the following statement of facts &c in the shape of a communication to the Hon. Secy. of War of the Confederate States, was presented by Mr. Wm. A. Little and unanimously adopted, Viz:

Fredsburg, Va., May 31, 1864.
    To the Hon. James A. Seddon,
    Secy. of War of the Confed. States
    Richmond, Va.

At a meeting of the Mayor & Common Council of Fred[erick]sburg., Va., held this 31st of May 1864, a Committee of the Citizens to wit, Montgomery Slaughter and John F. Scott, were appointed to repair to Richmond and present to you the following statement and application,

Statement.

On Sunday the 8th inst. a number of slightly wounded and straggling Federal Soldiers, who entered the Town, many of them with arms in their hands and with the capacity and intention we feared, of doing mischief in the way of pillage & injury to our people, who were unprotected by any Military force, were arrested by order of our Municipal authorities and forwarded to the nearest Military post as Prisoners of War. Under a guard of Citizens, these prisoners amounted to about 60 men of whom but few are said to have been slightly wounded. In retaliation for this act, the Provost Marshall, under orders from the Secretary of War in Washington, arrested on the 20th inst. some Sixty of our Citizens and forwarded them to Washington, to be held as hostages for said prisoners, ten of the[se] citizens were afterwards released in Washington & have returned to their homes, leaving some 57 citizens, still in confinement who have been sent to the Military prison at Fort Delaware.[3]

In behalf of these unfortunate people, who are thus made to suffer so seriously and for their suffering families, who are thus left without their natural protections and many of them without their means of support, we appeal to you to take such steps as may be proper &in accordance with Military regulations, to return the said prisoners to the Federal authorities and thus secure the release of our Citizens; Surely the matter of a few prisoners cannot be allowed to interfere with the human[e] and generous work of restoring to those desolated homes and those mourning women and children, the only source of comfort which the fate of War has left them, in this War ravaged and desolated Town, the prisoner of those loved ones, who are [now] separated from them and imprisoned at Fort Delaware.

The following is a list of the Citizens arrested and carried to Washington as aforesaid:

1. James H. Bradley–   Released at Washington
2. Thomas F. Knox   Ditto
3. James McGuire   Ditto
4. Counseller Cole   "

5. Michael Ames   "
6. John G. Hurkamp   "
7. John J. Chew   "
8. George H. Peyton   "
9. W[illia]m. H. Thomas   "
10. John D. Elder   "

---

1. F[rancis] B. Chewning
2. R.B. Reynolds
3. Jas. B. Marye
4. Geo. Aler
5. Charles Mander
6. Benj. F. Carrell
7. John L. Knight
8. Wm. C. Smith
9. Joseph W. Sener
10. E[dward] W. Stephens
11. Charles Cash
12. Charles B. Waite
13. Charles G. Waite, Jr.
14. Geo. W. Wroten
15. Thomas Newton
16. R.H. Alexander
17. Robt. Smith
18. L[ucien] Love
19. Geo. F. Sacrey
20. Henry M. Powers
21. L[andon] J. Huffman
22. Lewis Moore
23. John T. Evans
24. Walter Bradshaw
25. Saml. D. Curtis
26. Lewis Wrenn
27. William White
28. John Solan
29. Geo. W. Eve
30. James Mazeen
31. Abraham Cox
32. Wm. Brannan
33. James A. Taylor
34. A[rgulus] E. Samuel
35. Tandy Williams
36. Robert S. Parker
37. Christopher Reinz
38. Thomas T. Coleman
39. Patrick McDowell
40. Chs. Williams
41. William Cox
42. Walter M. Mills
43. Ths. S. Thornton
44. John Joice
45. John Minor
46. Richard Hudson
47. W[yatt] B. Webb
48. Alex. Armstrong
49. Wm. Wiltshire
50. Gabriel Johnston
51. Geo. Mullen
52. William Burke

The following Citizens were arrested subsequently and are still held by [the] Federal authorities.
1. William Lango

2. Thomas Manuell
3. Joseph Hall
4. William W. Jones
5. Wyatt Johnston

On motion of Messrs. M. Slaughter & John F. Scott were appointed a Committee to present the foregoing statement &c to the Hon. The Secy. of War of the Confed. States, the expenses of said Committee to be paid by [the] Chambn upon the order of one or more of the Finance Committee.

John Timberlake is appointed a Police Officer of this Corporation to date from the 28th May 1864.

On motion Messrs. J.H. Bradley, H.B. Hall & J.J. Young were appointed a Committee to collect for the use of the Corporation all the chloride of lime and other disinfecting agents left by the Enemy in this Corporation.

On motion, the Council then Adj[ourne]d.

M. Slaughter, Mayor

At a Called Meeting of the Common Council of the Town of Fred[erick]sburg, on the 13th day of June 1864–

Present–M. Slaughter, Mayor, Wm. A. Little, Recorder,
 Wm. H. Cunningham, H.B. Hall, J.J. Young,
 Jas. McGuire, B.T. Gill, James H. Bradley,
 Common Councilmen.

Messrs. M. Slaughter & Jno. F. Scott, the Committee heretofore appointed to report [repair] to Richmond & present the statement and application for the relief of our Citizens who have been arrested as hostages by the Enemy, and who are now confined at Fort Delaware, to the Secy. of War of the Confederate States, made a report in writing, And thereupon the following Resolution offered by Mr. J.J. Young, Viz: Resolved that the Council tender their thanks to Messrs. Slaughter & Scott for the faithful discharge of their duty in the premises from the time of their entering therein to the present period, was passed by the following Vote, Ayes– W.H. Cunningham, H.B. Hall, J.J. Young, Jas. McGuire, B.T. Gill, Jas. H. Bradley, 6 No—W.A. Little, who stated that he approved fully of the action of the Committee up to the time of their return to Fredericksburg, but that he disapproved of their subsequent action as unauthorized and as establishing a bad precedent.

On motion Ordered that the Agent for the sale of salt continue to dispose of the salt to the Citizens who have not been supplied at 13c per pound, and the balance at 25c pr. pound.

On motion, the Council then adjd.

M. Slaughter, Mayor

At a Called Meeting of the Common Council of Town of Fredericksburg, held on the 20th day of June 1864–

Present–M. Slaughter, Mayor,
        Wm. A. Little, Recorder,
        Wm. H. Cunningham, H.B. Hall, B.T. Gill, J.J. Young,
        James McGuire, L.B. Rose, Common Councilmen.

The Mayor stated that the Council had been called in order to receive and consider the Report of Mr. G.H.C. Rowe, of the result of his mission to Washington to effect the release of your Citizens, now in confinement as hostages at Fort Delaware, and thereupon Mr. Rowe made a report in writing as follows, Viz:

Fredericksburg, June 20th 1864.
Hon. M. Slaughter, Mayor &c.
Sir:
In discharged (sic) of the Commission Confided to me by the Municipal authorities to represent to the Federal authorities, the terms upon which the exchange of certain Citizens prisoners of Fredericksburg was proposed to be procured by consent of the Confederate Government. I have to report that I proceeded to the office of Col. H.H. Wells, Provost Marshal General of the defences (sic) South of the Potomac, at Alexandria, as the nearest Military post of the United States, with which I had opportunity of communicating. It was received and treated by that officer with all the consideration and delicacy consistent with the circumstances of my approach and finally furnish with a Passport to return and signify to the Confederate Government the assurance that the Authorities at Washington would unconditionally release the citizens captured at Fredericksburg when the soldiers taken prisoners by the Municipal officers were surrendered. They gave me authority to bring the prisoners referred to within their lines with the assurance of certainty that I should simultaneously receive the captured Citizens. I there-

fore propose that the Soldiers in question be delivered to you on parole, to be nullified & fulfilled, only when the citizens shall be forthcoming. This proposition it seems to me, obviates all difficulty of misconstruction, and I will undertake the delivery and receipt of the prisoners at Alexandria. It is proper to state, that in 1862 I undertook and executed a similar commission of exchange of Citizens captured, with success and thorough satisfaction to our Government and I am sure with its assent & cooperation as proposed, I will now reap a similar result.[4]

I am Sir, with the highest respect
truly yours
G.H.C. Rowe

Which report was on motion received & ordered to be filed, and on motion of Mr. Wm. A. Little, it was unanimously–

Resolved, That M. Slaughter, Mayor & G.H.C. Rowe, Esqr., be and they are hereby appointed Commissioners on the part of the Corporation of Fredsburg. to proceed to Richmond and urge upon the Confederate States Authorities to agree to the return of the Prisoners arrested in Fredsburg. either by parolling them subject to exchange for our Citizens Prisoners now in custody of the United States Authorities, or in any other way which may be agreed upon to effect the object, and whole subject is hereby referred to said Commissioners, with full authority to do every thing in the premises which in their Judgment they may deem necessary and proper to secure the release and return of our citizens to their homes.

On motion–Dr. J.G. Wallace, is appointed to attend any cases of Small pox in this Corporation and to take such steps as he may think necessary to prevent the spread of the disease. And that his bill for the same be paid by the Chamberlain.

M. Slaughter, Mayor

At a Called Meeting of the Common Council of the Town of Fredericksburg, held on the 27th day of June 1864–
Present–M. Slaughter, Mayor, Wm. A. Little, Recorder
James H. Bradley, H.B. Hall, J.G. Hurkamp, L.B. Rose,
J.J. Young and B.T. Gill, Common Councilmen
Messrs. M. Slaughter & G.H.C. Rowe, the Committee heretofore

appointed to proceed to Richmond & to urge upon the Confederate States authorities to agree to the return of the Prisoners arrested in Fredsburg. &c made a verbal report of the success of their mission and filed the following document as a part thereof, Viz:

Confederate States of America War Department
Richmond, Va.
June 23rd, 1864.
Brig. Genl. M.M Gardner,
Sir:
I will thank you to deliver to M. Slaughter, Mayor of Fredericksburg, fifty six Federal Soldiers (privates) who are to be exchanged for an equal number of our people captured in Fredericksburg. I will thank you also to furnish M. Slaughter the necessary guards &c for their transportation to Fredg. Please send two or three surgeons with the party.
    Respy. Yr. Obt. Svt. R. Ould, Agt. of Exchange
    Official J.H. Alexander
    Endorsed
    Head. Ins. Post Richmond June 23rd 1864
    B 409
    Resp. referred to Maj. Covington for the execution of the within order of Mr. Ould. By command of Brig. Genl. Gardner–E.A. Sample, Capt. & A.A.G.

Which report was on motion received.
    On motion of Mr. Wm. A. Little, Ordered that the Commissioners of exchange of Prisoners be and they are hereby authorized to employ two ambulances to be used in conveying the Federal prisoners now here up to Alexandria and all expenses attending the same, together with those incurred by said Comnrs. heretofore in affecting the exchange, be paid by the Chambn. upon the order of the Finance Committee.
    On motion, ordered that Jas. T. Kendall procure a voluntary Guard of 15 men to relieve the Guard now having the Federal soldiers in charge, during the coming night.
    On motion, the Council then Adjd.
                                                           M. Slaughter, Mayor

At a Meeting of the Common Council of the Town of Fred[erick]sburg, held on the 27th day of June [11th day of July], 1864,
Present–M. Slaughter, Mayor, Wm. A. Little, Recorder,
B.T. Gill, L.B. Rose, Jas. H. Bradley, H.B. Hall, J.G. Hurkamp, J.J. Young, Jas. McGuire, J.B. Sener.

The Mayor stated that the Council had been convened for the purpose of receiving the Report of Mr. G.H.C. Rowe, Comnr. for the exchange of Federal prisoners for our citizen prisoners confined at Fort Delaware,

Whereupon Mr. Rowe made a report in writing as follows, Viz:

Hon. M. Slaughter
Fredericksburg, July 8th, 1864
Mayor &c.

Sir:
I have the honor to report that I reached the Military lines of the United States in safety with the fifty six Federal prisoners of war, and four civil officers of the so called State of West Virginia. Committed to my charge by the Corporation authorities to be exchanged for the Captive Citizens of Fredericksburg after sum (sic) difficulty in obtaining personal access to the authorities at Washington and several days discussion there, I succeeded in closing a negotiation that the Federal prisoners delivered by me, should be released from their paroles simultaneously with the delivery of Fifty three Captive Citizens of Fredericksburg and seven confederate prisoners of war, on board a flag of truce steamer with transportation to Split Rock on the Potomac River. In the execution of this obligation the Federal authorities delivered to me, on board the Steamer Weycamoke, whence they were landed at Split Rock on yesterday fifty nine citizens & two prisoners of war, according to the roll which accompanies this Report marked A. The four citizens and five prisoners of war still due, I have solid assurance will be forwarded by the same route at an early day. In discharge of expenses, I have paid the sum of $366.83 in Federal Money & $ 70. in Confederate Money.

            Very Respy.
            G.H.C. Rowe

Which report having been read was on motion received.

On motion of J.J. Young, The thanks of this body be tendered to Mr. Rowe for energetic and efficient manner in which he has effected the Exchange of Federal Prisoners for our Captive Citizens.

On motion, the Council Adjd.

M. Slaughter, Mayor

At a Called Meeting of the Common Council of the Town of Fred[erick]sburg, held on the 18th day of July 1864–

Present–M. Slaughter, Mayor
      Wm. A. Little, Recorder
      J.G. Hurkamp, Jas. H. Bradley, W.H. Cunningham, Jas. McGuire, B.T. Gill, J.J. Young, H.B. Hall.

An account of B. Clark, acting Coroner, for holding an inquest on the body of Chs. Humphreys, Amtg. to $5. is allowed & ordered to be paid.

An account of Jas. T. Kendall for summoning an Inquest on the body of Chs. Humphreys, Amtg. to $3.00 is allowed and ordered to be paid.

An Account of Martha Stephens for board & lodging the Federal Guard of Citizens returned under flag of Truce, amounting to $80. is allowed and [ordered] to be paid.[5]

On motion, the Council then Adjd.

M. Slaughter, Mayor

At a Called Meeting of the Common Council of the Town of Fred[erick]sburg, held on the 5th day of August 1864–

Present–M. Slaughter, Mayor
      Jas. H. Bradley, J.G. Hurkamp, J.W. Sener, J.J. Young, L.B. Rose, James McGuire, [B.T. Gill], Common Councilmen

The Mayor stated that the Council had been called at the instance of two of its members, Whereupon Mr. J.J. Young stated the object to be, to consider the propriety of memorializing the Confederate Government to effect that a Military force be stationed here to protect the Citizens and their property from depredation by the Enemy, And thereupon on motion of L.B. Rose, it is Resolved that a Committee to consist of three be appointed by the Mayor, to draw up a Memorial as aforesaid, and report the same to the Council, at its next meeting, for its consideration.

The Mayor appointed Messrs. L.B. Rose, J.H. Bradley & W.A. Little the Committee under the foregoing Resolution.

Dr. J.G. Wallace, Physician appd. to attend small pox cases, made a report which was read and ordered to be filed, [the] resignation therein expressed received.

Ordered that the Account of Dr. J.G. Wallace amtg. to $564.00 which is allowed by the Council, be paid by the Chamberlain.

On Motion of Mr. J.W. Sener, the Council then Adjd., to meet at the Call of the Committee to prepare the Memorial to the Confd. Gov. &c.

M. Slaughter, Mayor

At a Called Meeting of the Common Council of the Town of Fred[erick]sburg, on the 13th day of August 1864–

Present–M. Slaughter, Mayor
> Wm. A. Little, Recorder
> H.B. Hall, Jas. W. Sener, Geo. W. Eve, L.B. Rose,
> Jas. H. Bradley, B.T. Gill, Common Councilmen

The Mayor stated that the Council had been called for the purpose of laying before it a communication received by him from Mr. Wellinghly Newton in the words following to wit "Linden August 9th 1864 My dear Sir: I send by Capt. Hammack's boat 100 bushels of wheat for the use of the needy of Fredericksburg and its vicinity. I leave the distribution entirely to your discretion with confidence that you will dispose of it to the best advantage (here the minutes were torn).

PAGE TORN–The following text is from the initial draft of the minutes

[M. Slaughter, Mayor

Whereupon on motion, It is Ordered **(torn)** hereby requested to acknowledge **(torn)** to tender to Mr. Newton, the th **(torn)** thus made by him.

On motion, Ordered **(torn)** by Mr. Newton, be turned over to the Overseers of the poor, to be appropriated by them as indicated by the letter of Mr. Newton. And the said O.P. are directed to report the manner in which the said donation has been distributed.]

SMOOTH COPY OF MINUTES RESUMES HERE

On motion, Ordered that the Street Committee be and they are hereby instructed to view the Canal & premises in the vicinity of Hurkamp's tannery and to take such steps as may be necessary to abate any nuisance which may be occasioned by the overflow of water or otherwise, in said vicinity.[6]

An Account of W. Wright for attending to the Town Clock, was on motion referred to the F. Committee, with instructions to settle the same upon the best terms they can.[7]

On motion the Council then Adjd.

M. Slaughter, Mayor

At a Meeting of the Common Council of the Town of Fredericksburg, held on the 5th day of October 1864–
Present–M. Slaughter, Mayor
    Wm. A. Little, Recorder
    James McGuire, W.H. Cunningham, Jas. G. Hurkamp,
    L.B. Rose, J.W. Sener, H.B. Hall, J.J. Young, B.T. Gill,
    G. W. Eve, J.H. Bradley.

(just here the minutes were torn)
PAGE TORN–the following text is from the initial draft of the minutes

[Upon the representation by Mr. J.M. Herndon, that he had lost the July coupons **(torn)** Corp. Nod. 14, 83 & 90, amounting to $33.00 **(torn)** to the sd. Herndon, the Amt. of $33.- **(torn)** any loss which she may sus **(torn)** payment. **(torn)** Resolved That Whereas it **(torn)** the Salt Agent has been **(torn)** Fredg. the salt belonging to this Corporation, and this Council wholly disapproving of this action as a violation of the law and an injustice to our own Citizens, do hereby direct the said Salt agent not to sell or deliver any of said Salt to anyone not a Citizen of the Corporation, and if necessary, the Mayor is directed to call this matter to the attention of the next Court of this Corporation.]

SMOOTH COPY OF MINUTES RESUMES HERE

On motion, Ordered that the Salt Agent be and he is hereby directed to deliver to the Citizens of the Town, Salt at the rate of 5 lbs. to each member of the family at the price of 25c per pound. Said delivery to be made between this date and the 20th day of October 1864.

An account of Sarah W. Wroten against the Corp. amounting to $520. was presented and on motion laid on the Table.

On motion, the Council then Adjd.

M. Slaughter, Mayor

At a Called Meeting of the Common Council of the Town of Fred[erick]sburg, held on the 19th day of October 1864–

Present–M. Slaughter, Mayor
        W.A. Little, Recorder
        L.B. Rose, W.H. Cunningham, Jas. W. Sener, G.W. Eve,
        Jas. H. Bradley, James McGuire

The Mayor stated the Council had been called for the purpose of receiving a Report from the Overseers of the Poor, as to the distribution of the Wheat received from Mr. W. Newton as a donation to this Corp. And thereupon Mr. Jas. H. Bradley President of the Board of O. Poor made a report showing the distribution of the sd. donation together with a list of the recipients. And it appearing by said Report that there is a balance of $1,431.00 in the hands of the sd. Prest., said balance was paid over by him to the Chamberlain.

Mr. Geo. Mullen was unanimously elected an O. Poor of this Corp. in the room & stead of Jno. L. Knight, who has departed this life.

On Motion of Mr. W.A. Little, It was unanimously Resolved that the thanks of this Council be and they are hereby tendered to Mr. James H. Bradley for the energetic & efficient manner in which he has performed the arduous duties imposed upon him as President of the Board of Overseers of the Poor for this Corporation.

An a/c of R.W. Hart, Comnr. of the Rev. for 6 mos. salary to the 16th Sept. 1864, amtg. to $250. was Ord. to be paid by the Chambn.

An a/c of Mrs. A.C. Aler agt. the Corp. for entertaining three Yankee Surgeons, Amtg. to $60 was on motion laid on the table.

Whereas as the Council in their former resolution may have done injustice to Mr. Smith the salt agent & upon further understanding & a full verbal report from the said agent in regard to his action & the instructions under the law giving him considerable discretion in disposing of the salt in certain contingencies, thereupon, Resolved, that the Council are now satisfied that the said salt agent had no disposition to violate the law or the instruction of the Council which may have been misunderstood by him, and they are willing and do hereby withdraw any censure of said agent, which may be implied in said former resolution.

On motion, the Council then Adjd.

M. Slaughter, Mayor

At a Called Meeting of the Common Council of the Town of Fred[erick]sburg, held on the 1st day of November 1864–

Present–M. Slaughter, Mayor
    W.A. Little, Recorder
    Wm. H. Cunningham, L.B. Rose, H[orace]B. Hall, J.W. Sener, J.J. Young, Jas. McGuire, B.T. Gill, J.G. Hurkamp.

The Mayor stated the Council had been called for the purpose of considering what amendments if any should be made in the Market laws–
And thereupon on motion of Mr. L.B. Rose, Ordered that the Clerk of the Council do prepare an Ordinance in accordance with the views expressed by the Council this day and report the same to the Council at its next meeting.

An a/c of Geo. P. King against the Corp., amounting to $800.00 was on motion laid on the table.

And then the Council Adjd. to meet on Thursday next at 4 o'clock P.M.

M. Slaughter, Mayor

At an Adjourned Meeting of the Common Council of the Town of Fred[erick]sburg, held on the 4th day of November 1864–

Present–M. Slaughter, Mayor
    Wm. A. Little, Recorder
    J.G. Hurkamp, Jas. W. Sener, Jas. McGuire, Wm. H. Cunningham, B.T. Gill & G.W. Eve, **Common Councilmen**.

There being no business transacted, the Council on motion **Adjourned**.

M. Slaughter, Mayor

At a Called meeting of the Common Council of the Town of Fred[erick]sburg, held on the 11th day of November, 1864–

Present–M. Slaughter, Mayor
    W.A. Little, Recorder
    James McGuire, G.W. Eve, W.H. Cunningham, J.W. Sener, H.B. Hall, Jno. J. Young, L.B. Rose, B.T. Gill, J.G. Hurkamp, Common Councilmen

The Mayor stated that the Council had been called for the purpose of considering an application to be made to the Confederate Government for relief from taxation. And thereupon on motion Mr. L.B. Rose, it was Resolved, That the Mayor and Thos. B. Barton, Esqr. be appointed a Committee on the part of this Corp. to present in Richmond either to the Secretary of the Treasury or to Congress, as may be deemed best, after consultation with our Representative & others there, An application to be prepared by a Committee duly appointed for said purpose, for relief of this Community from Confed. taxation, at the present time, and to do whatever they may deem best in the premises to effect that very desirable object.

Messrs. M. Slaughter, Wm.A. Little & Geo. F. Chew were appointed the Committee to prepare the Application referred to in the foregoing Resolution.

On Motion, Ordered that the Chamberlain of this Corporation do pay to John Coakley agent &c the sum of one Thousand dollars.

On motion, the Council then Adjd.

                                      M. Slaughter, Mayor

At a Called meeting of the Common Council of the Town of Fred[erick]sburg, held on the 19th day of November 1864–

Present–M. Slaughter, Mayor
    Wm. A. Little, Recorder
    Horace B. Hall, Wm. H. Cunningham, J.G. Hurkamp, Jas. W. Sener, G.W. Eve, James McGuire.

The Mayor stated that the Council had been called for the purpose of considering a communication recd. from T.B. Barton, Esqr. one of the Comme. on the part of the Corp. to present in Richmond an application for relief from Confed. taxation and the said communication having been read, on motion of Mr. Geo. W. Eve, It is Ordered that the application prepared by the Committee appointed at the last meeting of the Council & addressed to the Secretary of the Treasury of the Confederate States, be modified and addressed to the Congress of the Confed. States and that our Senator be requested & our Representative be instructed to use their influence in obtaining the relief sought for by said application.

On Motion, Ordered that Messrs. H. B. Hall, L. B. Rose & John J. Young be and they are hereby appointed a Committee to Audit, State and Settle the final accounts of the Relief Committee.

On Motion, Ordered that the Finance Committee be and they are hereby authorized to sell the $15000 of Confed. Bonds now held by this Corp. & place the proceeds of sale to the credit of the Corp.

On motion, the Council then Adjd.

M. Slaughter, Mayor

At a Called Meeting of the Common Council of the Town of Fred[erick]sburg, at the Mayors office on the 2nd day of December 1864–

Present–M. Slaughter, Mayor
  Wm. A. Little, Recorder
  L.B. Rose, B.T. Gill, Jas. W. Sener, J.G. Hurkamp,
  J.J. Young, G.W. Eve,
  Common Councilmen Messrs. J.J. Young, L.B. Rose & H.B. Hall, the Committee heretofore appointed to Audit, State and Settle the a/c of the Relief Committee made a report in the words & figures following to wit:
Fredericksburg, December 1st, 1864.
To the Common Council of Fred[erick]sburg,

We the Undersigned Committee appointed by the Council to examine the account of M. Slaughter, Treasurer of Fred[erick]sburg. Relief fund, beg leave to report that we have discharged that duty and certify that on the 20th day of October 1863, as will appear by Council proceedings of that date, there remained in the hands of the Treasurer ($101,130.46/100 dollars) One hundred and one thousand one hundred & thirty 46/100 dollars in Confederate Money, which has been disbursed as follows:

To Overseers of the Poor by order of Council	$20,000.00
"Chamberlain of the Corp. by order of Council	$25,000.00
"Invested in 7 pr. cent Confederate bonds by	

Order of Council (Trust Fund)	$50,000.00
"Paid to sufferers under direction of Council Committee	$ 6,099.15
"Balance in hands of Treasurer paid over to Geo. F. Chew, Chambn.	$ 31.31
	101,130.46

which closes & finally settles the account of the said M. Slaughter as Treasurer of the Fredg. Relief fund.

> Jno. J. Young
> L.B. Rose
> H.B. Hall

Which report was on motion adopted, confirmed & Ordered to be filed.

Jno. M. Herndon, Esqr. by note in writing resigned his Office as Common Councilman which resignation was on motion received.

The Council then proceeded to elect a member of the board to supply the vacancy occasioned by the resignation of Jno. M. Herndon, Esq., when Mr. Geo. Gravatt was duly elected.

On motion, Ordered that Wm.A. Little, John F. Scott & Geo. W. Eve be and they are hereby appointed a Committee, whose duty it shall be to confer with the Confederate States Assessor, in regard to the assessment of real Estate in Fredg. , [and] to consider the matter under the recent instructions from Secy. Trenholm and endeavor to agree with the Assessor upon the rate of [said] Assessment, in accordance with said instructions.[8]

On Motion, Ordered that the payment of the sum of Thirty seven hundred & fifty dollars, made to John Coakley, Agent &c by the Chambn. upon the order of W.A. Little of [the] Finance Committee be and the same is hereby ratified & confirmed.

Geo. Gravatt, member of the Council elect, appeared, was qualified before the Mayor & took his seat at the board.

On Motion, it was unanimously resolved that the thanks of the Council, be and is hereby tendered to M. Slaughter, Treasurer of the Relief fund, for the able and faithful discharge of the troublesome & laborious duties which devolved upon him as such officer.

On motion, Resolved that Thomas B. Barton, Esqr., be respectfully requested to appear before the Committee of the Congress of the Confederate States, and [to] represent this Corp. in the application for remission of taxes now pending before said bodies, and to do whatever he may think proper to aid in securing their reasonable wishes in the premises.

Mr. Geo. Gravatt was appointed a member of the Finance Committee in place of John M. Herndon, resigned.

On Motion, Ordered that the Clerk of the Council do correspond with the Clerk of the Council of the City of Richmond & obtain from him a copy of the Ordinances regulating the sale of provisions &c in the streets of the City of Richmond &c.

On Motion, Ordered that W. A. Little, Geo. W. Eve & J.J Young be and they are hereby appointed a Committee to represent to the Secy. of War of the Confed. States, the facts in regard to the action of Govt. Agents & others in the purchase & transportation of provisions &c from this Town to Richmond & to request from him the same protection against their said action which has been granted to the City of Richmond.

On motion, the Council then Adjd.

M. Slaughter, Mayor

At a Called Meeting of the Common Council of the [Town] of Fredericksburg, held at the Mayor's office on the 16th Dec. 1864–
Present–M. Slaughter, Mayor
    Wm. A. Little, Recorder
    G.W. Eve, Jas. W. Sener, L.B. Rose, J.J. Young,
    W.H. Cunningham, B.T. Gill, H.B. Hall, Common Councilmen

Wm. A. Little, Chairman [of the] Comme. appointed at the last meeting of the Council to confer with the C. States Assessor in regard to the assessment of real Estate in Fredsburg. &c made a report in writing which report having been read was adopted & Ordered to be filed, and the Clerk is directed to furnish a Copy thereof to the Assessor.

Mr. Wm. A. Little, Chairman of the Comme. appointed at the last meeting of the Council to represent to the Secy. of War of the Confed. States the facts in regard to the action of Govt. Agents & others in the purchase & transportation of provisions &c from this Town to Richmond, made a report in writing which report having been read, was adopted & ordered to be filed & the Clerk is directed to furnish a Copy thereof.

On motion Ordd. that the Chambn pay to the Police officers their Salaries for the quarter ending the 19th Instant.

On motion, the Council then Adjd.

M. Slaughter, Mayor

1865

At a Called Meeting of the Common Council of the Town of Fred[erick]sburg, at the Mayors Office on the 9th day of January 1865–

Present–M. Slaughter, Mayor
>Wm. A. Little, Recorder
>Geo. W. Eve, Wm. H. Cunningham, H.B. Hall, B.T. Gill, J.W. Sener, J.G. Hurkamp, John J. Young, Jas. McGuire, Common Councilmen.

The following Resolutions offered by Mr. Jas.W. Sener were passed, Viz:

1. Resolved, That the Corporation borrow from the Trustees of the Soldiers family Fund, the $50,000 of 7 per Cent Confederate bonds, now in their hands, and give to said Trustees their obligation to return, one year after the termination of the present war, an equal amount of the 8 per Cent bonds of the Confederate States, to said Trustees, and to pay semiannually to them the same interest which the said bonds so borrowed now yield.

2. That the said Trustees be requested to comply with the wishes of the Council, as expressed in the foregoing resolution.

3. That the Finance Come. of the Corporation be instructed to carry out the foregoing resolutions.

On Motion, Mr. Wm. H. Cunningham was appointed a member of the Finance Committee, during the absence of Mr. Jas. H. Bradley.

On Motion, Ordered that the Property Come. be & they are hereby authorized to permit Mrs. Martha Stephens to occupy & cultivate the Fair grounds, during the pleasure of the Council.[9]

On Motion of Mr. Wm. A. Little, Resolved That our Townsman Wm.S. Gillman, Esqr., be and he is hereby requested by the Council to give us the benefit of his influence & cooperation with T.B. Barton, Esqr., who was appointed heretofore, to press before the Members of Congress the application of this Corporation now pending there, for relief from Confederate States taxation.

On motion, the Council then Adjourned.

M. Slaughter, Mayor

At a Called Meeting of the Common Council of the Town of Fred[erick]sburg, at the Mayor's Office on the 11th day of February 1865–

Present–M. Slaughter, Mayor
   Wm. A. Little, Recorder
   H.B. Hall, J.J. Young, Geo. Gravatt, Jas. W. Sener,
   Wm. H. Cunningham, B.T. Gill, G.W. Eve, J.G. Hurkamp,
   Common Councilmen.

The Mayor stated [that] the Council had been called for the purpose of giving some expression of the high estimate in which our fellow Citizen Genl. Daniel Ruggles is held in this Community,

Upon motion, it was unanimously Resolved,

That this Council has recently with great pleasure greeted the return upon a short furlough of Brig. Genl. D. Ruggles, to his home in our midst. That they have observed with pride & pleasure his steady devotion to the Confederate cause, and his distinguished and arduous services in our Army for the past four years, and have seen with regret that Promotion in his case has not followed and rewarded his devotion to the Cause. Born in the Enemy's Country, but marrying a daughter of Virginia, and making his home among us, at the first call of the Southern War Trumpet, he resigned his Commission as Colonel in the Enemy's Army and all the fair prospects of rank and promotion, sacrificing property & family ties and tendered his sword to his adopted State, and among the first, if not the very first officer of the old Army who did so, with unswerving devotion has devoted his best efforts to the success of the Southern cause, after four years of arduous & valuable service he returns to us with the Rank of Brigadier General. The Council and the[this] whole community feel mortified to think, that an adopted son of old Fredericksburg should thus labour [labor] unrewarded, and that his distinguished services should be thus overlooked & unappreciated, and they respectfully present this case to the consideration of the Confederate authorities, in the confident trust that they will repair this unjustice & permit this War torn & loyal Town to rejoice in the reflection that the devoted loyalty & prompt and valuable services of Daniel Ruggles, are appreciated and honored by his adopted Country.[10]

Resolved, that a Copy of these Resolutions be respectfully forwarded to the President, Secy. of War & to Genl. R.E. Lee, Commander [in Chief] of our Armies & to Genl. Ruggles.

On motion, the Council then Adjd.

M. Slaughter, Mayor

At a Called Meeting of the Common Council of the Town of Fredericksburg, held at the Mayor's Office on the 27 day of Feby. 1865–
Present–M. Slaughter, Mayor
    Wm. A. Little, Recorder
    B.T. Gill, H.B. Hall, L.B. Rose, J.J. Young,
    Wm. H. Cunningham, G.W. Eve, J.B. Sener,
    Common Councilmen.

On motion of Mr. Wm.A. Little, It was resolved that George F. Chew, be and he is hereby recommended by the Common Council of Fredg. to the Commissioners appointed under the Act of February 1864, to distribute the fund coming to this Corp. for the relief of the indigent families of Soldiers & Sailors in the Confederate service, from Fredsburg. It is believed that Fredg. has furnished some 500 Soldiers & Sailors to the Country and there are now 82 families, many of them large & helpless, dependent upon this fund for bread.

The following Resolution was unanimously adopted:
Resolved That Messrs. G.H.C. Rowe & John F. Scott, be and they are hereby appointed by the Council to wait on the Military authorities of Fredsburg. and to respectfully request that the impressment of Corn or other provisions in a Community so destitute of supplies as ours, be suspended and that they earnestly protest against the reported impressment this morning and against any further action in that direction, looking toward such impressments[s], the Council being satisfied that the supplies in the Town are entirely insufficient for the supply of our own people and the poor depending upon them for bread.

On motion, the Council then Adjd.

                                    M. Slaughter, Mayor

At a Called meeting of the Common Council of the Town of Fred[erick]sburg, held at the Mayor's Office on the 1st day of [March] 1865
Present–M. Slaughter, Mayor
    Wm. A. Little, Recorder
    Geo. W. Eve, B.T. Gill, Geo. Gravatt, Wm. H. Cunningham,
    Jas. McGuire & H.B. Hall, Common Councilmen.

The following proceedings were had, Viz:

Whereas it has come to the knowledge of this Council that a large lot of tobacco, said to be 4,000 Boxes, part of which has already arrived, is about to be transported to and stored within the limits of this Corporation, under the control and by direction of certain officials of the Confederate Government, the manifest effect of which is to attract a raid of the Enemy upon us, involving more injury and destruction to our impoverished Citizens and their unfortunate town, for it will be impossible to conceal the fact from the enemy of this arrangement, is completed. This Council therefore being of opinion that a proper regard for their own interests & those of the Confederacy, require that they should communicate this information to the Secretary of War, that the Government may be fully advised of this proceeding, respectfully do so hereby.

And they further respectfully suggest, that if this be a bona fide Government transa[c]tion, its results may be disastrous to this Community in its present unprotected and exposed condition, and while we are prepared to do all things & to suffer all things which a proper regard for the public interests may demand of us as a loyal and law abiding community, we are unwilling to subject ourselves to unnecessary and useless exposure without adequate results in benefit to this Comn. - And we further respectfully suggest that a large brick fire proof house, owned by William Pratt, Esqr., within a mile of Hamilton's crossing, on the river, would be a better point to store and ship said Tobacco if it must take this direction, and its storage there would save costly transportation to this [the] Government, and perhaps avoid the dangers to us, which its deposit here so manifestly threatens.[11]

On motion, Resolved, That the Mayor be requested to communicate the foregoing proceedings as soon as possible, in such manner as he may think best.

On motion, the Council then Adjourned.

M. Slaughter, Mayor

At a Called Meeting of the Common Council of the Town of Fred[erick]sburg, held at the Mayor's Office on the 17th day of March, 1865–

Present–W[illia]m A. Little, Recorder

    B[everly] T. Gill, Geo[rge] Gravatt, John G. Hurkamp, John J. Young, Geo[rge] W. Eve, H[orace] B. Hall, W[illia]m H. Cunningham & Joseph W. Sener, Common Councilmen.

The Recorder stated that the Council had been called for the purpose of considering & passing upon such claims as may be presented against the Corporation.

The following claims were presented, passed & ordered to be paid, Viz:

 James T. Kendall $115.50
 Robt. W. Hart, Comnr. of Rev.   125.00

On motion, the Council then Adjd.

Wm. A. Little, Recorder

At a Meeting of the Common Council of the Town of Fred[erick]sburg, at the Court house, on Monday the morning of the 20th day of March 1865

Present–Wm. A. Little, Recorder

 J.J. Young, Jno. G. Hurkamp, J.W. Sener, James McGuire, G.W. Eve, H.B. Hall, B.T. Gill, Wm. H. Cunningham.

There not being a competent number present for the dispatch of other business, the members present ordered the polls to be opened, for the election of twelve Councilmen, this being the day fixed by law for that purpose, and the voters having cast their ballots, it was found on counting the same, that the votes were as follows, Viz: For Horace B. Hall 170, Wm. H. Cunningham 167, George Gravatt 167, John G. Hurkamp 161, John J. Young 150, Beverly T. Gill 148, G.W. Eve 144, Wm. A. Little 127, Jno. McGuire 127, Jas. W. Sener 103, Thos. F. Knox 76, Chs. S. Scott 70, Chs. Herndon 66, Peter P. Burr 58, Edward Carter 45, W.W. Spindle 36, Geo. Mullen 36, the first named twelve of whom were declared duly elected.

And then the Council Adjd.

M. Slaughter, Mayor

Council Chamber, March 21st 1865.

H[orace] B. Hall, Wm. H. Cunningham, Jno. J. Young, Jno. G. Hurkamp, B[everley] T. Gill, W.A. Little, Jas. McGuire, Jas. W. Sener, G.W. Eve & Geo. Gravatt, Thos. F. Knox,

 Members elect of the Common Council of the Town of Fredericksburg met at the Council Chamber and severally took the oaths of office before J.G. Wallace, Esqr., and Justice of the Peace for the Corporation of Fred[erick]sburg.

On motion Jas. McGuire was called to the Chair.

The Salary of the Mayor was fixed at One thousand dollars.

The Council then proceeded to the election of a Mayor, when M. Slaughter was elected and took the several oaths of office before J.G. Wallace, a Justice of the Peace for the Corporation of Fredsburg.

Mr. W.A. Little was duly elected Recorder of the Corporation and took the oaths of office before M. Slaughter, a Justice of the Peace for the Corporation of Fredericksburg.

On motion the Salaries of the following officers were fixed as follows:

The Clerk [of the Council at]–Two hundred dollars

The Chamberlain of the Corporation at Eight hundred dollars.

The Commissioner of the Revenue at Five hundred dollars.

The Collector of Taxes & Rents at five per cent on the amt. [Amount] collected.

Geo. F. Chew was elected Clerk of the Council & Chamberlain of the Corporation.

R.W. Hart was elected Commissioner of the Revenue.

L.J. Huffman was elected Collector of Taxes & Rents.

[Jas. G. Read was elected Surveyor]

Robt. W. Hart was elected Inspector & Measurer of Lumber, Wood &c and Weigher & Measurer of Coal, Grain, Salt, &c.

On motion, The number of Police officers for the current year was fixed at two and their salaries were fixed at Five hundred dollars each per Annum.

The Council then proceeded to elect Police officers for the current year, when James T. Kendall & John Timberlake were elected on the first ballot.

Tax on Drays, Carts & Wagons for the present year was fixed at following [as follows], Viz: On drays & carts $30.– and on Wagons $60.–

The Mayor appointed the following [Standing] Committees for the current year, viz:

On Finance –Wm. A. Little, W. H. Cunningham & Chs. Herndon.

On Public Property –J.G. Hurkamp, James McGuire, Geo. Gravatt.

On Streets –Jas. W. Sener, Thos. F. Knox & Chs. S. Scott.

On Pumps –H.B. Hall, J.J. Young, B.T. Gill.

Mr. George W. Eve resigned his office as a member of this board, which resignation was on motion received.

The Council then proceeded to elect a member to supply the vacancy occasioned by the resignation of Geo. W. Eve, when Chas. Herndon, Esqr.

was unanimously elected, And thereupon the said Chas. Herndon appeared, was qualified before the Mayor & took his seat at the board.

On motion, Ordered that the Street Committee be and they are hereby instructed to take immediate steps, to have the marsh on the west of the town thoroughly drained.

On motion of Mr. Wm. H. Cunningham, Resolved, That the Council deeming it necessary to the health of the Town, do earnestly request the Citizens of the Town to have their cellars opened and cleaned out, and also their lots cleaned and kept in as good order as possible, and that the Police officers be instructed to publish notices to this effect.

On motion of Mr. Jas. W. Sener, Ordered that the a/c of Mrs. Ann E. Aler & Geo. W. Wroten heretofore laid on the table, be referred to a Come. to be appointed by the Mayor.

The Mayor appointed Messrs. Jas. W. Sener, Wm. H. Cunningham & Chs. Herndon, the Committee under the foregoing order.

On Motion, the Council then Adj[ourne]d.

M. Slaughter, Mayor

At a Called Meeting of the Common Council of the Town of Fred[erick]sburg, held on the 5th day of April 1865–

Present–M. Slaughter, Mayor
    Wm. A. Little, Recorder
    Jas. W. Sener, James McGuire, Chs. Herndon, Geo. Gravatt, J.J. Young, W.H. Cunningham, Tho[ma]s F. Knox, H.B. Hall, Common Councilmen.

James G. Read, who has been elected Surveyor of the corporation, appeared and took the oath [of] office before the Mayor.

Whereas the Military authorities have withdrawn from the Town and left the community in an unprotected situation & liable to Trespass and annoyance from straggling soldiers & other lawless persons and our Police force of two persons are manifestly insufficient in this emergency - Therefore on motion, Resolved that the Mayor be and he is hereby authorized to call upon the Citizens of the Town, when in his opinion occasion may require it, to act as a voluntary Police force, and to enroll their names as such, and the Citizens are earnestly requested to respond at once to said call, in order to secure the peace, protection and good order of the Community.[12]

On motion, the Council then Adjourned.

               M. Slaughter, Mayor

At a Called Meeting of the Common Council of the Town of Fredericksburg, held at the Mayor's Office on the 27th day of April 1865–

 Present–M. Slaughter, Mayor
    Wm. A. Little, Recorder
    John J. Young, Charles Herndon, James McGuire, Jas. W. Sener, Wm. H. Cunningham, B.T. Gill, Geo. Gravatt, Jno. G. Hurkamp, Thos. F. Knox, H[orace]B. Hall, Common Councilmen.

Chs. S. Scott, a member of the Council elect, appeared, was qualified before the Mayor & took his seat at the board.

On motion of Mr. J.J. Young, It is ordered that a Committee to consist of three be appointed by the Mayor, whose duty it shall be to draft Resolutions expressions of the sense of the Council in regard to our present situation, and to report the same to the Council this afternoon at 4 o'clock.

The Mayor appd. Messrs. Charles Herndon, John J. Young and Wm. H. Cunningham, the Committee under the foregoing resolution.

On motion, the Mayor Mr. M. Slaughter was added to the Committee.

On motion, the Council adjd. till 4 O'clock this afternoon.

               M. Slaughter, Mayor

At an Adjourned Meeting of the Common Council of the Town of Fredericksburg, held at the Mayor's office on Wednesday afternoon April 27th 1865–

 Present–M. Slaughter
    Wm. A. Little, Recorder
    Chs. Herndon, Geo. Gravatt, J.W. Sener, H.B. Hall, W.H. Cunningham, Chs. S. Scott, B.T. Gill, J.G. Hurkamp, James McGuire, J.J. Young, Thos. F. Knox.

The Committee appointed to draft Resolutions expression of the sense of this Council in regard to our present situation reported Resolutions, which report was on motion received and laid on the table.

The following preamble and resolutions were unanimously adopted, Viz:

Whereas this Community finds itself after four years of desolating War, all of whose evils and sacrifices they have been called on to endure, subject to the Government & laws of the United States, and under the control of its authority, and whereas they are satisfied that the War is at an end, and that their interests and duty alike require that they shd. recognize the situation and submit to said Authority & laws, and as quiet & orderly Citizens they acknowledge the powers that be, and endeavor to preserve that character of a law abiding & peacable community, which it has been their purpose to maintain, And Whereas further, it is deemed proper that this Community through their constituted representatives, give expression at this time to those views and communicate the same to the United States Authorities, Therefore, Resolved–

1. That M. Slaughter, Esq., be and he is hereby appointed a Commissioner to proceed to Richmond and present a Copy of these proceedings through Genl. M. R. Patrick to said Authorities.[13]

2. Trusting that as this Community and State is in no way responsible for the Causes which led to the Revolution, and have already suffered so seriously during its progress, a magnanimous Government will be satisfied with the restoration of its Authority and adopt towards us the policy of leniency & conciliation, which will tend with the people of Virginia, to restore friendly relations, soften the asperities and heal the wounds of the past and enable us to resume our former position as peaceful and prosperous Citizens of Virginia and the United States.

Resolved, that the crime of assassination which has so recently deprived the United States of its President has in all ages & Countries received the unqualified detestation of humble and Civilized Communities, and that the perpetration [perpetrator] of this crime deserves the utmost punishment of the law and the condemnation of all upright men.

On motion, the Council then Adjd. to meet Tomorrow Morning at 10 o'clock.

M. Slaughter, Mayor

At an Adjourned meeting of the Common Council of the Town of Fredericksburg, held at the Mayor's Office on the 28th of April 1865–
Present–M. Slaughter, Mayor
    Wm. A. Little, Recorder
    Charles Herndon, W.H. Cunningham, Jas. W. Sener, J.J. Young, B.T. Gill, H.B. Hall, Jno. G. Hurkamp, Jas. McGuire, Chs. Scott, Geo. Gravatt, Thos. F. Knox,
    Common Councilmen.

Mr. J.J. Young moved a reconsideration of the Preamble and Resolutions relating to our present situation, adopted on yesterday, which motion was unanimously carried, And thereupon on motion of Mr. W.A. Little, the following Preamble & Resolutions were unanimously adopted, [Viz:]

Whereas this Community finding itself subject to the Government and laws of the United States, and under the undisputed control of its authority, and Whereas they are satisfied that their interests and duty alike require that they should recognize the situation and submit to said authority and laws, and as quiet and orderly Citizens, acknowledge the powers that be, and endeavor to preserve the character of a law abiding and peaceable Community, which it has ever been their purpose to maintain, and Whereas further it is deemed proper that this Community through their constituted representatives, give expression to these views at this time, and communicate the same to the United States Authorities–Therefore, Resolved

1. That the Mayor, M. Slaughter, Esqr. be and he is hereby appointed a Commissioner to proceed to Richmond and present a Copy of these proceedings through Genl. M.R. Patrick to said Authorities.

2. Trusting that as this Community is in no way responsible for the causes which led to the Revolution, and have already suffered so seriously during its progress, a magnanimous Government will be satisfied with the restoration of its authority and adopt toward us the policy of leniency and conciliation, which will tend with the people of Virginia, to restore friendly relations, soften the asperities and heal the wounds of the past, and enable us to resume our former position as peaceful and prosperous Citizens of Virginia and the United States.

3d. Resolved that this Community in common with the whole Southern people, believing that the crime of assassination which has so recently deprived the United States of its President, has in all ages and Countries, received the unqualified detestation of honorable and civilized communities, hereby express their hearty condemnation of the said crime and their profound regret that it should have been committed.[14]

On motion, the Council then Adj[ourne]d

M. Slaughter, Mayor

At a Called Meeting of the Common Council of the Town of Fred[erick]sburg, at the Mayor's office on Tuesday the 2d day of May 1865–

Present–M. Slaughter, Mayor
    W.A. Little, Recorder
    Wm. H. Cunningham, J.W. Sener, B.T. Gill, Chas. Herndon, H. B. Hall, C.S. Scott, Jno. J. Young, Geo. Gravatt, Jas. McGuire, Thos. F. Knox, J.G. Hurkamp,
    Common Councilmen.

M. Slaughter, [Esq.,] Mayor, made a verbal report of the result of his mission to Richmond, under resolutions of the Council adopted on the 28th of April 1865, and thereupon on motion of Mr. T.F. Knox, It was unanimously

1. Resolved, That in the Judgment of this Body, in the situation in which we are now placed, it will be proper and manifestly the duty as it is clearly the interest and policy of our Civil authorities, to take the Oath of Amnesty and allegiance to the United States Government, thus securing the preservation of our Civil rights, and as speedily as possible resuming our de facto position as Citizens of the United States.

Resolved, That the Mayor and Council and Civil Officers of the Corporation of Fredericksburg, will in a Body take said Oath before Col. Sumner, Commanding Sub. District of the Rappahannock.[15]

On motion, the Council then Adjourned.

M. Slaughter, Mayor

Editor's Note:

Following defeat of the Confederate armies, Federal forces not assigned to occupation duty marched toward Washington D.C., crossing the Rappahannock River over the course of two weeks in mid-May. Some of the corps marched through town, while others marched around, crossing on pontoon bridges at Franklin's crossing, downstream of Fredericksburg and on pontoons at United States Ford, which lay upstream. Of interest is the Union 20th Corps, which included the troops who had comprised the 11th Corps in the Army of the Potomac. They crossed the river at U.S. Ford, near where they had met disaster at Chancellorsville. Their road back to that vicinity had included transfer to the west, where they had fought at Chattanooga and in the Atlanta campaign, marched with Sherman to the sea, and then pursued Confederate forces through the Carolinas. The Fredericksburg Ledger described the interchange between conquering armies and the civilian population, as follows: "The troops behaved, as far as we have heard, with great propriety, as they passed through. Pies, biscuits, and edibles were prepared and sold to them by the citizens, who in this way collected together a good deal of small change." The article also noted that Generals Sherman and and Meade "surveyed the old battle grounds with much interest."[16]

At a Called Meeting of the Common Council of the Town of Fred[erick]sburg, held at the Council Chamber on Wednesday the 14th day June 1865–

Present–M. Slaughter, Mayor
    Wm. A. Little, Recorder
    Thomas F. Knox, Jas.W. Sener, Chas. Herndon, Chs. S. Scott and B.T. Gill, James McGuire, John G. Hurkamp.

After a verbal statement made by the Mayor, On motion of Mr. Jas. W. Sener, It was Resolved that M. Slaughter, Mayor, W.A. Little & Chs. Herndon, be and they are hereby appointed a Committee to draft resolutions to be presented to his Excellency Gov. Peirpont [Pierpoint] (sic), setting forth our present situation &c and on his further motion, the subject of having the obstructions &c in the River removed was referred to the same Committee, with directions to take such action as they [to them] may see[m] necessary to effect that object.[17]

On motion, the Council [then] Adjd.

                                 M. Slaughter, Mayor

Council Chamber
Fredericksburg, July 20th, 1865.

James McGuire, B.T. Gill, Thomas F. Knox, Chs. S. Scott, J.G. Hurkamp, John J. Young, W. A. Little, H.B. Hall, Jas. W. Sener, and George Gravatt & Wm. H. Cunningham, members of the Common Council elect, of the Town of Fredericksburg, met at the Council Chamber and took the oaths of office before G.F. Chew, a Notary Public for the Corporation of Fredericksburg.

On motion, James McGuire was called to the Chair and W.H. Cunningham was appointed Clerk pro tem.

On motion, The Salary of the Clerk of the Council was fixed at $2 for each Session of the Council.

Geo.F. Chew was elected Clerk of the Council, was qualified & entered upon the discharge of his duties as such.

The Salary of the Mayor was fixed at $200 to the 3rd Monday in March next.

M. Slaughter was unanimously elected Mayor of the Corporation and took the several oaths of office before Wm. H. Cunningham Comn. [and acting] under a Commission from the Governor of Virginia.

Jas. W. Sener was elected Recorder of the Corporation and took the oaths of office before M. Slaughter, a Justice of the Peace for the Corp. of Fredsburg.

The Salaries of the following officers were fixed as follows.

The Chamberlain of the Corp. at the rate of Four hundred dollars per Annum.

The Commissioner of the Revenue at $250. for the balance of the year.

The Collector of Taxes & Rents at 2 per cent on all Taxes collected by him to the 1st of October & 5 pr cent on Taxes recd. thereafter & 2 per Cent on Rents.

Geo. F. Chew was elected Chamberlain.

[Robert W. Hart, was elected Commissioner of the Revenue.

_____ was elected Collector of Taxes & Rents

Carter M. Braxton was elected Surveyor]

Robert W. Hart was elected Inspector & Measurer of Lumber, Wood &c.

Lewis Layton was elected Weigher & Measurer of Coal, Grain, Salt &c.

On motion, The number of Police officers for the current year was fixed at two and their Salaries were fixed at the rate of $150.00 each per Annum.

The Council then proceeded to elect Police Officers for the current year, when James A. Taylor & John [S.]G. Timberlake were elected on the first ballot.

The Tax on Drays, Carts & Wagons for the present year, was fixed as follows, Viz: On Drays & Carts $5.- and on Wagons $10.

Absent, M. Slaughter, Mayor.

On motion, James McGuire was called to the chair.

On motion, the Vote by which the Salary of the Mayor was fixed at $200 for the balance of the year was reconsidered.

On motion, The Salary of the Mayor was fixed at the rate of Four hundred [dollars] per Annum.

The Mayor appointed the following Standing Committees:

On Finance–Wm. A. Little, W.H. Cunningham & Chas. S. Scott

On Public Property–James McGuire, H. B. Hall, C. Herndon

On Streets–Jas. W. Sener, Jno. G. Hurkamp, Geo. Gravatt

On Pumps–B. T. Gill, John J. Young, Thomas F. Knox

Robert W. Hart, James A. Taylor, John S.G. Timberlake took the Oaths of Office before the Mayor.

On motion, the Council then Adj[ourne]d.

M. Slaughter, Mayor

At a Called Meeting of the Common Council of the Town of Fred[erick]sburg, held at the Mayor's Office on Tuesday Evening the 1st day August 1865–

Present–M. Slaughter, Mayor
    B. T. Gill, W.H. Cunningham, Jas. McGuire, John J. Young, Chs. S. Scott, J.G. Hurkamp, Geo. Gravatt,
    Common Councilmen.

The Official bond of Geo. F. Chew as Chamberlain of this Corp[oration] in the penalty of $10,000 with John F. Chew & John G. Hurkamp as Securities, was presented to the board, approved and ordered to be filed with the Mayor, to be taken care of by him, in the best manner he can under existing circumstances.

Chs. Herndon, Member of the Council elect appeared was qualified before the Mayor and took his seat at the board.

On motion, Ordered that a Committee of three be appointed, whose duty it shall be to enquire into the right and expediency of Taxing by the Corp. Stages, Carriages & all other Vehicles running on the Streets of the Town at the same rate that Drays and Carts & Wagons are now taxed, And the said Committee are directed further to enquire and ascertain whether the Charter of the Rd. Fredg. & Potomac Rail road Company has expired and if so, what rights heretofore granted to said Company by the Corporation reverts to the Corp. by reason thereof.

The Mayor appointed Messrs. Chs. Herndon, W.A. Little & Chs. S. Scott, the Committee under the foregoing order, with directions to report.

An A/c of M. Slaughter against the Corp. amounting to $18.75 was presented, allowed and ordered to be paid by the Chamberlain.

The following Communication was presented by the Mayor, Viz: "Fredericksburg, Va., Aug. 1st, 1865. Mayor Slaughter, The Sanitary Condition of your Town will of course claim the first and earnest attention of your Council. I am desirous of Cooperating, so far as I am able in this matter, and desire the co-operation of the City authorities in return. It will be indispensible to have labor, which cannot be procured without money. I would therefore suggest that you take into consideration the propriety of levying a small per capita and also property tax for this purpose.
I am Gentlemen, Very Respectfully, Yours,
T.M. Harris, Brig. Genl."[18]

Which communication having been read was ordered to be filed and on motion, The Mayor is requested to reply to said communication.

The Council proceeded to elect a Collector of Taxes & Rents of the Corporation, when L[andon] J. Huffman was unanimously elected.

The following persons were elected Overseers of the Poor for the Town, to serve until the next annual appointment, Viz: Chs. S. Scott, Edwin Carter, E[dward] L. Heinichen, Geo.W. Wroten, Chs. B. Waite & Wm. Burke.

L[andon] J. Huffman, Collector &c. took the oaths of office before the Mayor.

The Official bond of L[andon]J. Huffman as Collector of Taxes & Rents in the penalty of $10,000 with W.P. Conway & W.H. Hill as Securities, was presented to the board, approved & ordered to be filed with the Mayor, to be taken care of by him, in the best manner he can under existing circumstances.

On motion, Ordered that a Committee of two be appointed whose duty it shall be to enquire and report to the Council what alterations & amendments are necessary to be made in the Ordinances of the Corporation, in relation to colored persons.

Messrs. Charles Herndon & W.A. Little were appointed the Committee under the foregoing order.

On motion, The Mayor was added to the foregoing Comm.

On motion, Ordered that the Finance Comm. be instructed to require the Comnr. of the Revenue forthwith to proceed and list all persons doing business in this town & who are subject to license tax, and the said Comm. are directed to prepare a tax bill in conformity with such list & to report the same to the Council, at the earliest day practicable.

James B. Sener, W.A. Little and John F. Scott are appointed Proxies to represent the interests of the Corporation in the Fredg. & Gordonsville Rail Road Company, at any meeting of the Stockholders of the said Company to be held hereafter.[19]

On motion, the Council then Adjourned.

M. Slaughter, Mayor

At a Called Meeting of the Common Council of the Town of Fredericksburg, held at the Council Chamber on Tuesday the 8th day of August, 1865–

Present–M. Slaughter, Mayor
    J.W. Sener, Recorder
    Wm. H. Cunningham, Chas. S. Scott, B.T. Gill, Chs. Herndon, James McGuire, Jno. J. Young, J.G. Hurkamp, Common Councilmen.

On motion made and seconded, It is ordered that the Chamberlain be and he is hereby directed to purchase [fourteen] chairs for the use of the Council & of the Corp. Court, upon the best terms that he can.

An Ordinance imposing taxes for the year 1865, was passed & is in the words & figures following to wit:

An Act imposing Taxes for the 1865
Passed August 8th, 1865

1. Be it ordained by the Mayor & Common Council of the Town of Fredericksburg, that there shall be levied and collected on persons, property and all other subjects of the Town of Fredericksburg to defray the expenses of the Corporation for the year ending the third Monday in March 1866, the Taxes following, to wit:

2d. On Real Estate, forty [fifty] cents on every hundred dollars value thereof, agreeably to the Commissioners Books.

3. On all personal Property forty [fifty] cents on every hundred dollars Value thereof, agreeably to the Commissioners Books.

4. On each white or colored male above twenty one years of age, Two dollars.

5. On monies solvent bonds and securities and liquidated claims, except the bonds of the Corporation, forty [fifty] cents on every hundred dollars.

6. On all Capital invested or used in any manufacturing business or invested used or employed in any trade or business, Twenty five cents on every hundred dollars.

7. On the monies and personal property of Joint Stock Companies forty [fifty] cents on every hundred dollars.

8. On a license to keep an ordinary or house of public entertainment, thirty [forty] dollars, and if the yearly value of such house & furniture exceeds $100. and is less $200. &c.

NOTE: *The official minutes of the August 8, 1865 meeting end abruptly here, with a garbled Item 8. The draft minutes, however, continue with all of the specific taxes enumerated in the minutes of August 21, below. As a consequence, there is no point in repeating that list here. For the taxes shown in the August 21 minutes, the initial tax proposed on August 8 is shown in brackets.*[20]

And on motion, the Council then Adjourned.

M. Slaughter, Mayor

At a Called Meeting of the Common Council of the Town of Fred[erick]sburg, at the Council Chamber on the 21st day August 1865–
Present–M. Slaughter, Mayor
Jas. W. Sener, Recorder
W.A. Little, James McGuire, Chs. S. Scott, W.H. Cunningham, B.T. Gill, Geo. Gravatt, Chs. Herndon, H.B. Hall, Common Councilmen.

The Mayor stated that the Council had been convened for the purpose of considering a Communication addressed to J.W. Sener, Esqr. Recorder, by Geo.H.C. Rowe, Esqr., Chairman of a Committee appointed at a Public Meeting of the Citizens of Fredericksburg protesting against the Tax bill lately passed by the Common Councilmen, And also a communication from Capt. Herman Siligson, Provost Marshal, regarding the Sanitary condition of the Town, Which Communications were read and Ordered to be filed–And thereupon on Motion of Mr. Wm.A. Little,

It was Resolved, That an appropriation of _ dollars be made, to be expended under the direction of the Street Committee, in cleaning the lots, streets & alleys of the Town, in conjunction with the Military Authorities and that the Ordinance Chap. 38 be at once strictly enforced by the Police Officers, except that the Owners or Agents of vacant lots shall be required to remove all necessaries at once, and the same shall be removed by the Police and the expenses charged to said Owners and recovered by Warrant in case said parties fail to obey said Orders.

On motion of Mr. H[orace] B. Hall the blank in the foregoing Resolution was filled with the sum of Five hundred dollars by the following Vote; Viz: Ayes. Wm. A. Little, James McGuire, C.S. Scott, B.T. Gill, Geo. Gravatt, Chs. Herndon, H[orace] B. Hall, 7—Noes. J.W. Sener, W.H. Cunningham.

Ordered that the Clerk of the Council do cause a Copy of the foregoing Resolution to be presented to the Military Authorities of the Town.

On motion the tax Bill passed by the Council on the 8th day of August 1865 was taken up for reconsideration & amendment, And thereupon the following Tax bill was read & passed in lieu of the bill passed the 8th day of August, 1865, Viz:

An Act imposing Taxes for the [year] 1865
Passed August 21st 1865.

1. Be it Ordained by the Mayor & Common Council of the Town of Fredericksburg, That there shall [be] levied and collected on persons property & other subjects of the Town of Fredericksburg to defray the expenses of this [the] Corporation for the year ending the third Monday in March 1866, the taxes following, to wit:

2. On Real Estate, forty [fifty] cents on every hundred dollars value thereof agreeably to the Commissioners Books.

3. On all Personal property, forty [fifty] cents on every hundred dollars value thereof agreeably to the Commissioners Books.

4. On each White or colored male, above twenty one years of age, Two dollars.

5. On Monies, solvent bonds, securities and liquidated claims, except the bonds of the Corporation, forty [fifty] cents on every hundred dollars.

6. On all Capital invested or used in any Manufacturing business, or invested, used or employed in any Trade or business, Twenty five cents on every hundred dollars.

7. On the monies and personal property of Joint Stock Companies forty [fifty] cents on every hundred dollars.

8. On a license to keep an Ordinary or house of Public Entertainment Twenty [forty] dollars, and if the yearly value of such house and furniture exceeds one hundred dollars and is less than Two hundred dollars, the Tax shall be twenty five [fifty] dollars, and if the yearly value exceeds Two hundred dollars, there shall be added to the last mentioned sum, five [ten] per centum on so much thereof as exceeds Two hundred dollars.

9. On a license to keep a house of private entertainment, or [a] private boarding house, or any other house not private, but kept for public resort for any purpose, five dollars [$10.], and if the yearly value of such house & furniture exceed One hundred dollars, there shall be added to the last mentioned sum, five [ten] per centum on so much thereof as exceeds One hundred dollars. [But no house shall be deemed a private boarding house with less than five boarders.]

10. On every license to keep a Cook Shop or eating house, Seven dollars and fifty cents [$15.00], and in addition thereto, five [ten] per centum on so much of the yearly value thereby [thereof] as exceeds One hundred dollars.

11. On every license permitting a Bowling Alley or Saloon, Twenty [forty] dollars, provided that where there is more than one such Alley kept in any one room, Seven dollars & fifty cents [$15] each shall be charged for the excess over one.

12. On every license permitting a Billiard table, Thirty seven dollars & fifty cents [Seventy five dollars], provided that where there are more than one such Table kept in any one room, fifteen [thirty] dollars each shall be charged for the excess over one table.

13. On every license permitting a Bagatelle or other like Table, Twelve dollars & fifty cents [Twenty five dollars], and if more than one, five dollars [$10] for each additional table kept in the same house.

14. On every license to a Keeper of a Livery Stable, one dollar for each stall thereof.

15. On every license to a Merchant or Mercantile firm, if the Capital employed, including as Capital the Cash so used, whether borrowed or not, and goods purchased on credit by the Merchant or firm, be shown by affidavit, to be less than $500, the tax to be paid shall be ten [twenty] dollars; if over $500 & under $1,000, fifteen dollars [$30]; if $1,000 & under $1,500, Seventeen dollars & fifty cents [$35]; if $1,500 & under $2,500, Twenty dollars [$40]; if $2,500 & under $5,000, Thirty dollars [$60]; if $5,000 & under $10,000, fifty dollars [$100]; if $10,000 & under $15,000, Sixty five dollars [$130]; and if $15,000 & under $20,000, Seventy five dollars [$150]; and in every case in which the license to a Merchant or Mercantile firm includes permission to sell wine, ardent spirits, or a mixture thereof, porter, ale or beer by wholesale or retail, an additional tax of Twenty [Thirty] dollars, subject however to a deduction of the amount of taxes imposed on this Class by the Military Authorities.

16. Merchant Tailors, lumber merchants, dealers in coal, ice or wood, shall obtain licenses as Merchants and be assessed and Taxed thereon as other Merchants are by the preceding section of this act.

17. On every license to a Commission Merchant, forwarding Merchant and Ship Broker, Twenty [forty] dollars each.

18. On every license to an Auctioneer or Vendue Master, Twelve dollars and fifty cents [Twenty five dollars], and one per cent on [upon the amount of] all sales made by him on them.

19. On every license to a person selling goods by sample or card otherwise than at some store house or place of trade, Fifty dollars, but such sales made at such store house, shall subject the person doing business at such storehouse to a tax, required to be paid by a Merchant.

20. On Hucksters, Pedlars & others, vending articles in the Streets or elsewhere in the Town, whether of Foreign or domestic growth and manufacture, Twenty five dollars.

21. On every license permitting any public show, exhibition or performance $10.~; and for every exhibition of a Circus $20.~; And for every exhibition of a Menagerie $30.~; All shows, exhibitions and performances, whether under the same canvas or not, shall be construed to require a separate license therefor; And upon any such shows, exhibitions or performances being concluded, so that an additional fee for Admission be charged, the same shall be construed to require an additional license therefor.

22. On every license to an Agent or Sub-agent of any Insurance Company not chartered by this State, Twenty five dollars.

23. On every license to the owner of a Daguerrean or such like gallery, by whatsoever name it May be known or called, Twelve dollars & fifty cents [Twenty five dollars].

24. On every license to sell by retail, Porter, Ale or beer, Twenty dollars.

25. On every license to a Broker, Twenty five [Fifty] dollars.

26. On every license to a person engaged as agent for the renting of houses & lands, ten dollars.

27. On every license to a person engaged as agent for renting [selling] and purchasing real estate, Twelve dollars & fifty cents [Twenty five dollars].

28. On every license to a Physician, Surgeon or Dentist, and on every license to an Attorney at law, five dollars.

29. On every Steamboat agent, fifty dollars for each Steamer for which he may be an agent.

30. On Toll Bridges and Ferries, Ten [Twenty] dollars.

31. Be it further ordained, That the Commissioner of the Revenue do extend in the books, provided for the [purpose], the amount due from each person under the provisions of this Ordinance.

32. Be it further Ordained, That the said Commissioner of the Revenue shall assess all persons required to obtain licenses, and make a fair alphabetical list thereof, as far as he may have progressed with the same at intervals not exceeding fifteen days, and deliver such list to the Collector for his guide in collecting the Taxes imposed by this Ordinance on such licenses.

33. Be it further Ordained, That all persons who shall call on the Collector and pay him the taxes due by them under this ordinance (except license tax) by the 15th of December next, shall be entitled to a deduction of five per centum, & those paying by the 15th day of January next to a deduction of two per centum, on the amount of their respective accounts.

34. Be it further Ordained, That the taxes shall be collected, accounted for and paid to the Chamberlain of the Corporation by the Collector from time to time as collected, and [that] the said Collector shall finally settle his collections on or before the Second Monday in March next.

35. Be it further ordained, That the said Collector shall not be allowed to return any lists of insolvents or absentees or have any credit therefor but upon oath in affirmation that such list is true, nor shall such return be admitted by the Chamberlain in his settlement with the Collector, until the same be passed upon and allowed by the Common Council.

This Act shall be in force from its passage.

The following Resolution offered by Mr. Wm. A. Little was adopted:

Resolved, That the Finance Committee be requested to report to the Adjourned meeting of the Citizens of Fredericksburg on the Tax bill; that the Council have carefully reconsidered the Tax bill, and all the objections made thereto by the Committee appointed by the said meeting; [And] though they very much fear that the bill as amended, will not raise the funds necessary to be raised for the necessary expenditures of the Corporation, Yet in deference to the expressed wishes of the people in said meeting, and in the earnest desire to reduce the taxes to the lowest point in the present condition of our community, the Council has reduced the bill.

On the application of Mr. James R. Dowell, leave is granted him to extend his Telegraph lines through the Town during the pleasure of the Council, and under the Supervision of the Street Committee.

On motion, Mr. Chas. S. Scott as an Overseer of the Poor is requested to attend specially to the case of Jeremiah Allen, a Citizen of the Town.

On motion, The 8th Section of the 25th Chapter of the Ordinance licensing Drays, Carts & Wagons, is amended so as to read: The rates of hauling shall be forty cents for Drays & Carts and eighty cents for wagons, per load to and from the wharves, until changed or altered by an ordinance.

Mr. H.B. Hall tendered his resignation as a Member of the Council, which was on motion received.

The Council then proceeded to fill the vacancy occasioned by the resignation of Horace B. Hall, when Robt. W. Adams was unanimously elected.

On motion, the Council then Adjourned.

M. Slaughter, Mayor

At a Called meeting of the Common Council of the Town of Fredericksburg, at the Council Chamber, on Monday the 28th of August 1865–

Present–M. Slaughter, Mayor
  Jas. W. Sener, Recorder
  John J. Young, Thos. F. Knox, Chs. Herndon, Chs. S. Scott, James McGuire, Wm. H. Cunningham, B.T. Gill,
  Wm. A. Little, Common Councilmen.

An account of C.S. Scott against the Corp. Amounting to $19.30 is allowed & ordered to be paid.

The Mayor presented to the Board a Communication from Geo. H.C. Rowe, Chairman on the part of a Meeting of the Citizens of Fredg. accompanied by a copy of the Resolution passed by said Meeting, which communication having been read, was on motion, recd. And thereupon the following Resolutions were adopted, Viz:

Resolved that in reply to the Resolutions of the Adjourned meeting of the Citizens of Fredericksburg, the Council respectfully states that they fixed the Salaries of the Corporation officers at a former meeting, and by law they have now no further control over the matter. That they have reduced the tax bill as far as they can do with any Regard to their sworn duty; And that it is not possible further to reduce said bill and carry on the organization of the Corporation.

On motion, the Council then Adjourned.

M. Slaughter, Mayor

At a Called Meeting of the Common Council of the Town of Fred[erick]sburg, at the Council Chamber on the 8th day of Sept[ember] 1865–

Present–M. Slaughter, Mayor
        Jas. W. Sener, Recorder
        C.S. Scott, John J. Young, Chs. Herndon, J.G. Hurkamp, Jas. McGuire.

Robt. W. Adams, member of the Council elect, appeared, was qualified before the Mayor and took his seat at the board.

An a/c of Hart & Hayes Amtg. to $0.80c is allowed & ordered to be paid.[21]

Ordd. that the account of Buddy Taylor for cleaning out and liming the Exchange Hotel amtg. to $5.00 is allowed & Ordd. to be paid—And it is further Ordd that the Mayor proceed to receive the said amt. from the Exchange Hotel Company under the Ordinance in that case made and provided.

Present–Wm. H. Cunningham.
On motion, Jas. McGuire was excused.
Messr. Chs. S. Scott tendered his resignation as an Overseer of the Poor of this Corp. which resignation was on motion received.

Mr. Charles B. Waite tendered his resignation as an Overseer of the Poor of this Corp., which resignation was on motion received.

Messrs. James Hayes & Argalus E. Samuel were elected Overseers of the poor of this Corp. in the room and stead of Chs. S. Scott & Chs. B. Waite, resigned.

On motion, the Council then Adjd.

M. Slaughter, Mayor

At a Called Meeting of the Common Council of the Town of Fred[erick]sburg, at the Council Chamber on Saturday the 16th day of Sept[ember] 1865–

Present–M. Slaughter, Mayor
> Jas.W. Sener, Recorder
> Chs. S. Scott, W.H. Cunningham, Thos. F. Knox,
> John J. Young, James McGuire, Wm. A. Little, Chs. Herndon, R.W. Adams,

The following preamble & Resolutions were on motion unanimously adopted, Viz:

Whereas the Common Council of the Town of Fredericksburg have reason to believe that the Animus and principles of their people have been misrepresented to the people and Government of the United States, Therefore,

1. Be it Resolved by this body, that personally as well as in the name and on behalf of the people of Fredericksburg, we claim for them and hereby declare that by our voluntary and prompt acceptance of the Oath of Amnesty and Assumption of the obligations of Citizenship we have signified our intention and now reiterate our determination to bind the State of Virginia to the Federal Union, believing that in that Union lies all her interests and all her hopes of prosperity.

II. Resolved, That the forbearing and conciliatory course of President Johnston (sic), and his wise and magnanimous statesmanship, claim our admiration, confidence & grateful appreciation, and that we recognize in his co-laborer in the work of the restoration of the South, Hon. F.H. Peirpoint (sic), Governor of Virginia, an Officer equal to the arduous task before him, and whose Administration calls for this recognition of its ability and success.[22]

III. Resolved, that we take this occasion to testify our appreciation of the able, impartial and courteous character of the Military Administration of Major Genl. S.S. Carroll, Commanding this District, that we recognize his successful efforts to Administer justice & promote harmony among all Classes, and in our opinion, the interest of the Government will be subserved by his continuing in command at this place.[23]

4. Resolved, that the Mayor be requested to communicate a copy of these proceedings to Maj[or] Gen[era]l Terry, commanding Department of Va. thru Major General S.S. Carroll, commanding this District.

Ordered that the a/c of E. McDowell against the Corp. Amtg. to $11.50 be paid by the Chamberlain.

On motion, M. Slaughter is appointed Proxy to represent the interests of the Corp. at any meeting of the Stockholders of the Fredg. and Gordonsville Rail Road Co. in the place of John F. Scott, who declines to act.

On motion, An additional appropriation of $250. is made, to be expended by the Street Committee.

On motion, Ordd. that the Public Property Comme. cause the wall around the Grave yard on Pr. Edwd. Street to be repaired & put in order.[24]

On motion, the Council then Adjd.

            M. Slaughter, Mayor

At a Called meeting of the Common Council of the Town of Fredericksburg, at the Council Chamber, on Friday the 22d day of September 1865–

Present–M. Slaughter, Mayor
    Jas. W. Sener, Recorder
    Chs. Scott, Charles Herndon, James McGuire, B. T. Gill, George Gravatt, Wm. H. Cunningham, John J. Young.

The Mayor presented a communication from the Street Committee which being read, on motion made and seconded, the same was referred to a committee consisting of Charles Herndon, Wm.H. Cunningham & William A. Little, with directions to said committee to report upon the subject matter of said communication to an adjourned meeting of the Council, to be held at four & a half O'clock tomorrow afternoon.

On motion, the Council Adjourned.

            M. Slaughter, Mayor

At an Adjourned meeting of the Common Council of the Town of Fredericksburg, held at the Council Chamber on Saturday the 23d day of September 1865–

    Present–M. Slaughter, Mayor
        J.W. Sener, Recorder
        James McGuire, Charles S. Scott, Wm. H. Cunningham,
        John J. Young, Charles Herndon, B. T. Gill.

    Charles Herndon from the committee appointed on yesterday to consider & report upon the communication of the Street Committee presented on yesterday, made a report which was read and adopted, and is as follows, Viz:

    Whereas the Corporation of Fredericksburg in the [its] original grant to the Richmond Fredericksburg & Potomac Rail Road Company expressly stipulated that, in
laying the rails across the streets the said Company shall not be allowed to form any inconsistent
[inconvenient] obstruction to the passage of carriages along the street[s], across the said railroad, nor to obstruct the passage of the water through the gutters of the said streets. And whereas said Company lately rebuilt its Bridge over the Rappahannock river at this place and in such rebuilding it has without the consent of the Corporation authorities elevated said Bridge and by consequence its track through the Town, thereby in the opinion of the Street Committee and other citizens, forming inconvenient obstructions to the passage of carriages across said streets, And whereas the culverts and [other] means of drainage on or near Princess Anne Street, are in the opinion of the same Committee in such condition as not effectually to drain the water from the streets and lots adjacent thereto. And whereas Col. Carter M. Braxton the Engineer Agent of the said Company states in person before the Council that he is instructed by said Company, so to grate [grade] the streets as will in his opinion do away with any and all obstructions so complained of or likely to be complained of. And that he is instructed also [so] to open and clean out the culverts and other means of drainage at the points complained of as effectually to drain the streets and lots adjacent thereto. Now this Council not desiring to act in any captious spirit, but only to preserve intact the rights of the Town, are willing at the instance of the said Engineer Officer, to await the result of said grading and cleaning, which in the opinion of said Engineer will remedy the said grievances, of course this delay is without prejudice to

This brick wall along the western edge of Hurkamp Park is what survives from the period when the park was the Corporation Burying Ground.

the rights of the Town, in the premises, and said Company will have to reimburse any and all individuals who may be injured or damaged by the work already done or that which is to be done. Should said grading when completed satisfy the said Street Committee that said track as it then stands forms no inconvenient obstruction to the passage of carriages across said track, and should said cleaning effectually drain the streets and lots now complained of, then this Council will be satisfied that no damage will result to the Town from the present elevation of said track, But should the said grading and cleaning not effectually remedy the grievances complained of, then this Council will proceed at once against said Company to enforce the legal rights of the Town in the premises.[25]

Resolved, that a Copy of these proceedings be sent to the President of said Company.

On motion, the Council then Adjourned.

M. Slaughter

At a Called Meeting of the Common Council of the Town of Fredericksburg at the Council Chamber on Monday Afternoon, October the 23[rd], 1865–

Present–M. Slaughter, Mayor
    Jas. W. Sener, Recorder
    Chs. Herndon, Wm. H. Cunningham, Chs. S. Scott,
    Geo. Gravatt.

There being no quorum present, the Council stood Adjourned.

M. Slaughter, Mayor

At a Called Meeting of the Common Council of the Town of Fred[erick]sburg, held at the Council Chamber on Tuesday Evening, October 24th, 1865–

Present–M. Slaughter, Mayor J.W. Sener, Recorder James McGuire, Robt. W. Adams, Chs. S. Scott, W. H. Cunningham, B.T. Gill, J.G. Hurkamp, Geo. Gravatt, J.J. Young, Chs. Herndon, Common Councilmen.

The Mayor having reported in writing that the Police Officers had discharged their duties for the last quarter, as well as could be expected under the circumstances, it is ordered that the Chambn. pay them their Salaries for said quarter.

An Account of Johnston & Co. for lamps & kerosene oil Amtg. to $4.75 is allowed and ordered to be paid.

On motion, Ordered that the Chambn. pay to Robt. W. Hart $93.75, amt. of his Salary as Comnr. of the Revenue for the quarter ending the 20th Inst.

The Civil War era bridge had been built on stone piers, one of which is visible on the bank of the Rappahannock River. The concrete railway bridge just upstream remains in use.

An a/c of Jno. J. Berry against the Corp. amtg. to $11.00, was on motion referred to the Finance Com. for settlement.

On motion of [Mr.] Chs. Herndon, Esqr., Resolved that the quarters Salaries of the Corporation officers due March 1865, be paid at the rate of 23 for 1 in specie or its equivalent.

A Motion was made by Mr. Chs. Herndon, that the Salaries of Corp. officers from the 3d Monday in March 1865 to the 20th July 1865 be paid at the rate of 60 for 1 in specie or its equivalent, and the vote being taken on sd. motion it was rejected.

Messrs. Jas. B. Jones & M. Slaughter [M. Slaughter & Jas. B. Sener], Proxies to represent the Corp. at any meeting of the Stockholders of the

Fredericksburg and Gordonsville Rail road Company made a report in writing, which report having been read was on motion received and ordered to be filed.

On motion of Mr. Chs. Herndon the following preamble and resolution was adopted, [Viz]

Whereas a Memorial has been addressed to the Mayor and Commonalty of the Town of Fredsburg from Messrs. C.S. Kewell and John E. Vassar, asking for the use of the armory room in the court house building, for the purpose of instructing white children of the Town, whose parents & Guardians may be unable to pay for tuition.

Resolved that the use of the said [room] be granted to said applicants for the period of twelve months for said purpose, the necessary repairs to be made without expense to the Corp. as proposed in the memorial of the said applicants.

An application in writing from Hugh S. Doggett, proposing to rent the main building of the Town Hall, was on motion referred to the Public Property Committee, with instructions to said Comm. in any arrangement[s] made with the applicant, to keep in view the thorough repair of the Building, in order to the preservation of that property.

On motion of Mr. James McGuire, It is ordered that the Chamberlain be & he is hereby directed to cause a notice to be served on the Sergeant of the Corporation of Fredsburg requiring him to pay over to the said Chamberlain the amt of a Judgment received [recovered] by the Mayor & Commonalty of said Town against the Old Dominion Steam boat Company.

On motion, the Council then Adjourned.

M. Slaughter, Mayor

At a Called Meeting of the Common Council of the Town of Fredericksburg, held at the Council Chamber on Thursday evening the 9th day of November 1865–

Present–Jas. W. Sener, Recorder
       James McGuire, Geo. Gravatt, W.A. Little, W. H. Cunningham, Chs. Herndon, B. T. Gill, Chs. S. Scott, Jno. G. Hurkamp, Jno. J. Young.

The Chambn reported to the Council, that in Obedience to an order heretofore entered he caused a notice to be served on the Sergt. of this Corp requiring him to pay over to sd Chambn for the use of the Corp. the amt. of a Judgment in favor of the Corp. against the Old Dominion Steam boat Company and that the said sergeant has [had] failed to do so as required.

An Account of Messrs. Waite & Sener, amounting to $66.50 as Certified by the Corp. Court for payment, is allowed & Ordd. to be paid by the Chambn. Mr. Chs. Herndon moved that the Sergt. of this Corp. be directed to pay over the amt. of the Judgt. recovered by the Corp. against the Old Dominion Steam boat Company to Messrs. Wm. A. Little & Chs. T. Goolrick, the Council of the Corp. in said case, Which motion Mr. Cunningham moved to amend to the effect that said Sergt. be directed to pay over one moiety of sd. Judgt. to Mr. Wm. A. Little and that he pay over the other moiety thereof to the Chambn. for the use of the Corp., and the vote being taken on said Amendment, it was carried.

An application of Mr. James B. Ficklen, proposing to purchase the fee simple Estate in an house & lot on Caroline Street, was on motion referred to the Commt. on Public Property, with directions to report to the Next Council.

Mr. Wm. A. Little of the Finance Committee, to whom was referred the Account of Mr. John J. Berry, amounting to $11.00 reported adversely to the payment of sd. a/c, [which] report was concurred in.

On motion of Mr. James McGuire, The Recorder Mr. Jas. W. Sener, is requested to confer with the Freedmens Bureau, and ascertain their views, with regard to the appointment of an Agent on the part of the Citizens of the Town, to act in conjunction with said Bureau in all cases in which white & colored persons are concerned.[26]

On motion of Chs. S. Scott, It is Ordd. that a Comm. to consist of three be appd. by the Mayor whose duty it shall be, to confer with the Fredg. Aqt. Co. and inform them of the reasonable complaints of the people of the Town, growing out of the mismanagement of the affairs of said Company and request that a General meeting of the said Company be called to confer with said Committee, & also to ascertain at what sums said Company will dispose of their works to the Corporation, and to report the result of their conference to the Council.[27]

The Mayor appointed Messrs. Chs. S. Scott, Jno. G. Hurkamp & J.W. Sener, the Committee under the foregoing order.

On motion, the Council then Adjd.

M. Slaughter, Mayor

At a Called Meeting of the Common Council of the Town of Fredericksburg, at the Council Chamber, on Tuesday Evening the 14th day of Novr. 1865–

Present–M. Slaughter, Mayor
        Jas. W. Sener, Recorder
        R.W. Adams, James McGuire, Wm. H. Cunningham,
        Chs. Herndon, Chs.S. Scott, J.G. Hurkamp, B.T. Gill,
        Thomas F. Knox, Common Councilmen.

Ordered that the a/c of James H. Bradley, amounting to $86.00 which is allowed, be paid by the Chambn.

The Fredericksburg Court House, built in 1852, was used by the Freedmen's Bureau after the war. St. George's steeple is on the left, with the municipality's clock visible just above the tree.

On motion, Ordered that the Clerk be & he is hereby authorized to purchase stationary for the use of the Council & for official purposes, the account for the same to be rendered to the Council for its approval.

On motion of Mr. Chs. Herndon, Resolved, That the Council, in response to the proposition of the Steam Boat Company to remove the wrecks from the c[h]annel of the river near the Town, provided the Council would agree to pay for the Coal to be used in the experiment, hereby signify their willingness to furnish the Coal necessary provided not more than $60. worth of Coal will be required or used, to be pd. by the Chambn. upon the order of the Finance Committee; And should the first experiment succeed, then the Finance Committee are authorized to make a further expenditure in Coal, to remove the other wrecks, Said further expenditure not to exceed the sum of $150., the [this] Additional expenditure to be paid by the Chambn. on the order of said Committee.[28]

The Public Prop. Comm. to whom was referred the application of Mr. James B. Ficklen to purchase the fee simple estate in a house & lot on Caroline Street, reported adversely to said application, which report was on motion received & adopted.

On motion, the Council then Adjd.

M. Slaughter, Mayor

At a Called Meeting of the Common Council of the Town of Fred[erick]sburg, at the Council Chamber on Tuesday Evening the 5[th] day of December 1865–

Present–M. Slaughter, Mayor
    Jas.W. Sener, Recorder
    Chs. S. Scott, James McGuire, Geo. Gravatt, J.G. Hurkamp, Wm. H. Cunningham, John J. Young, B.T. Gill,
    Common Councilmen.

The Mayor stated that the Council had been convened for the purpose of considering the propriety and necessity of appointing a Citizen of the Town to act in conjunction with the Freedmans Bureau, when Mr. Chs. S. Scott moved that such appointment be now made, which motion was Carried-

The Council then proceeded to elect a Commissioner on the part of the Citizens of the Town in the Freedman's Court about to be organized, when James B. Sener, Esqr. was unanimously elected.

On motion, The Mayor was authorized to employ Council to protect the interest of the Corp. in the Suit now pending in the Circt. Court of Spots. County, under the style of Timberlake vs. Little & Co.

On motion, Ordered that the Chambn. pay the Insurance quota now due to the M.A. [Society of Va.] Security Co. amounting to $101.77.[29]

On motion of Mr. C.S. Scott, Ordered that the Mayor be & he is hereby requested & authorized to correspond and ascertain on what terms a sufficient Fire apparatus for the use of the Town can be procured.

On motion of Mr. J.J. Young, Resolved that the Mayor be requested to issue his Proclamation calling the Citizens together at an early day for the purpose of organizing a Fire Company.

Mr. J.W. Sener offered the following resolution, Viz:

Resolved, that from and after this day, a Tax of 5c upon every passenger passing through the Town upon the Richd. Fredg. & Poto. Rail Road, be imposed, and that said Company be liable to said Tax, which resolution was on motion of Mr. Jas. McGuire, laid on the table.

On motion, the Council then Adjd.

M. Slaughter, Mayor

At a Called Meeting of the Common Council of the Town of Fred[erick]sburg, at the Council Chamber, on Friday Evening the 15th day of December 1865–

Present–M. Slaughter, Mayor
        Joseph W. Sener, Recorder
        John G. Hurkamp, Wm. H. Cunningham, Geo. Gravatt,
        Wm. A. Little, James McGuire & B.T. Gill,
        Common Councilmen.

The Mayor stated that he had convened the council at the instance of the Recorder, who desired to submit a report in relation to the Fire Engines belonging to the Corporation, Whereupon on motion made & seconded, It was Resolved that J. W. Sener be appointed a Committee to proceed to Richmond and ascertain, whether the Fire Engine now in said City, is the property of the Corporation of Fredericksburg, and if so to take the necessary steps to procure it, and the said Joseph W. Sener is hereby invested with full power to sell & dispose of the said Engine if in his judgment it would be better to do so looking to the interests of the Corporation.

The stairs next to the Town Hall/Market House are still in place, but not safe to us.

The Mayor stated that he had in obedience to the request of the Council, employed Mr. Thomas B. Barton as council in the case against The Old Dominion Steam Boat Co., his compensation to be fixed hereafter by the Council by request of Mr. Barton.

The Mayor read a communication from W.R. Morse, Brvt. Major U.S.A. & Asst. Comnr. of Freedmen, Whereupon it was resolved that permission be granted the [said] Morse to occupy one of the rooms in the Court house for the purpose of holding a Freedmans Court.

On motion, Ordered that the Committee heretofore appointed to confer with the Fredg. Aqueduct Co. in relation to the management of said Co. be requested to examine into the present condition of the works of the Company and report to the Council.

The following bills were presented and ordered to be paid:

A.A. Little, New Era	$14.25
J.B. Sener, Ledger	16.00

Whereas the attention of the Council has been called by the Grand Jury of Inquest of this Corporation to the filthy condition of the Market house lot and the steps leading down from Princess Anne Street to the Market house, On motion ordered that the Public Property Committee be instructed to wait upon the officer commanding this Post and respectfully request him to have the Market House now occupied by the Troops vacated, as it is very much needed for Corporation purposes, and to further represent that the condition of the premises is caused (as the Council believe) by the occupation of said building by the soldiers.

Whereas the Grand Jury of Inquest of this Corporation has found the burnt walls on the Farmers Hotel lot to be very dangerous and should be removed. Therefore Resolved, that the Police Officers be directed to notify the owner thereof, to remove the same without delay; And if the said nuisance be not removed in three days, after notice to said owner, then the Police officers are hereby directed to remove the same at the expense of the owner to be recovered by warrant.

On motion made and seconded, Resolved that the Mayor be requested to confer with Mr. A[lexandria] K. Phillips in relation to the interests of the Corporation under the will of the late Mrs. Margaret Phillips and report the result of his conference to the Council.

On motion, the Council then Adjd.

M. Slaughter, Mayor

At a Called Meeting of the Common Council of the Town of Fredericksburg, held at the Council Chamber on the 28th day of December 1865–

Present–M. Slaughter, Mayor
    J.W. Sener, Recorder
    C.S. Scott, R.W. Adams, B.T. Gill, Jas. McGuire, J.G. Hurkamp, Geo. Gravatt, Wm. H. Cunningham, J.J. Young.

An a/c of B[erry] Peyton Amtg. to $1.50 is allowed and ordered to be paid by the Chambn.

Mr. J.W. Sener who was heretofore invested with full power to sell & dispose of the Fire Engine in the City of Richmond, made a report, which was read, recd & ordd. to be filed.

An a/c of J.W. Sener amtg. to $16.25 is allowed & ordd. to be paid.

The Committee heretofore appointed to confer with the Fredg. Aqt. Co. in relation to the management of said Company made a report in writing, which having been read was on motion ordd. to be filed.

Mr. Chs. Herndon resigned his seat as a member of the Council, which resignation was on motion received.

The Council then proceeded to elect a member to supply the vacancy occasioned by the resignation of Mr. Chs. Herndon when Mr. Jno. L. Marye, Jr. was elected on the first ballot.

A communication from Thos. B. Barton, Esqr., relating to the case of the Corp. Fredg. vs The Old Dominion Steam boat Co. was received & on motion ordd. to be filed.

On motion made & seconded, ordered that the several Communications recd. by the Mayor & now held by him, on the Subject of purchasing Fire Engines, be turned over to the Commander of said Company in the Town of Fredg.

On motion of Mr. J.W. Sener, Ordered that the Mayor be & he is hereby requested to direct the Comnr. of the Revenue to complete & furnish to the collector of Taxes his books for 1865, as soon as possible, and in the event of his inability to procure blank books to prepare them himself.

Mr. Jno. L. Marye, Jr., having declined to serve as a member of this body, the Council proceeded to elect a member in the room & stead of Charles Herndon resigned, when Mr. G.W. Shepherd was elected on the first ballot.

Present–Thomas F. Knox

Mr. J.J. Young moved the following Resolutions, Viz:

1. Resolved, as a the sense of the Council that the interest of this Corp. in the Fredg. & Gordonsville Railroad Co. be given to any Company or Corporation that will agree with the President & Directors of the sd. road to furnish the said [road] in five years from the first day of January next.

2. Resolved that the Delegate in the Legislature be requested to present this action to the Legislature and urge similar action by that body.

And the vote having been taken on said Resolutions by ayes and noes, they were adopted by the following vote, Viz: Ayes–J.W. Sener, Chs. S. Scott, J.G. Hurkamp, W.H. Cunningham, Jno. James Young, Geo. Gravatt–6

Noes–R.W. Adams, B. T. Gill, Jas. McGuire, Thos. F. Knox.

On motion then the Council Adjourned.

M. Slaughter, Mayor

NOTES

Newspaper references are noted where applicable. General biographical information was taken from *The Civil War Dictionary,* by Mark M. Boatner, III (New York: David McKay Co., 1959) and from *Historical Times Illustrated Encyclopedia of the Civil War,* Patricia L Faust, ed. (New York: Harper & Row, 1986). Newspaper references are noted where applicable.

1. From March through July of 1862, the Union Army of the Potomac operated on the Virginia Peninsula in an attempt to capture Richmond. In April, a supporting Federal force arrived in Fredericksburg, which disrupted local affairs and caused thousands of enslaved persons to leave their place of bondage.
2. Edward Heinichen's reminiscences are presented in Volume 6 of Fredericksburg History and Biography (2007). The Town Council's minutes related to the 1862 incident can be found in Volume 12 (2013).
3. The minutes suggest a great wrong visited on the citizens of Fredericksburg, but it was a crisis of their own making, as Edward Heinichen makes clear. Fort Delaware had been a coastal defense installation for decades, but had been reconstructed in stone shortly before the Civil War. When the Fredericksburg citizens were held there, several thousand other prisoners were there as well.
4. Henry H. Wells commanded the 26th Michigan Regiment, which was an occupation force. After President Lincoln was shot, he played a role in the pursuit and capture of John Wilkes Booth.
5. Martha Stephens lived in a house that fronted on Sunken Road. She is buried nearby. Both the house site and the grave are within the Fredericksburg and Spotsylvania National Military Park.
6. John G. Hurkamp was a local businessman and member of the Town Council. His tannery stood on the south side of William Street, where it is intersected by the modern day Littlepage Street. On December 13, 1862, during the first battle of Fredericksburg, Federal troops had occupied the brick structure and knocked out bricks to provide loopholes for musketry. Confederate artillery on the heights to the west (modern day University of Mary Washington) drove them away. On May 3, 1863, during the second battle of Fredericksburg, a Federal column advanced up William Street, but received severe artillery fire where the street crossed a drainage canal (the "Canal" referred to here). Several men

fell into the ditch and there well may have been corpses to be removed when the Street Committee was given the task of cleaning up the area.
7. Fredericksburg's town clock is located within the steeple of St. George's Episcopal Church. The church was constructed in 1849 and a clock placed in its steeple in 1851. It consisted of a central clock works that connected to four clock faces, one in each side of the steeple. The mechanical works had become worn out by the 1990s and the four clock faces no longer reflected the same time. The City of Fredericksburg, still responsible for its maintenance and upkeep, upgraded it to an electronic version.
8. George Alfred Trenholm, of Charleston, South Carolina, had been a successful businessman before the war, strongly supported secession, and subsequently made a fortune through his control of a fleet of blockade runners. He had unofficially advised the Confederate government treasurer since 1861 and had become Confederate Treasury Secretary himself in July 1864.
9. The fairgrounds had been the scene of a terrible slaughter during the December 13, 1862 battle of Fredericksburg.
10. Daniel Ruggles had been born in Massachusetts in 1810. He attended West Point, class of 1833, and fought with the U.S. Army in the Seminole Wars and the War with Mexico. In 1841, in Detroit, Michigan, he married Richardetta Mason Hooe, who had strong family ties to Fredericksburg. When the Civil War came, Ruggles resigned his commission and sided with the South. His greatest day in Confederate service occurred at Shiloh, but he did not fully impress his superiors and he spent the better part of the war handling administrative duties. He died in 1897. He and his wife are buried in the Fredericksburg City Cemetery.
11. The Pratt house, known as Smithfield, was a prominent landmark near the lower crossing, where elements of the Union army established a crossing in December 1862 and again in April/May 1863. It survived the war and is currently owned and used by the Fredericksburg Country Club. At the time of the Civil War, it was owned by Dr. Thomas Pratt, but the reference in the Council minutes is of a William Pratt. There was a William C. Pratt who owned a prominent house near Port Royal during the Civil War and it appears that another William Pratt constructed Smithfield around 1820.

12. At war's end, the absence of military authority and struggling local governments left many areas without civil authority. A certain lawlessness prevailed. On May 18, 1865, newly arrived military authorities in Fredericksburg announced that, "for the information and perfect understanding of all concerned, it is hereby ordered, that all Guerrillas, Horse-Thieves and Marauders, caught in the act, be shot on sight (Fredericksburg Ledger, June 10, 1865)."
13. Major General Marsena Rudolph Patrick had been the Provost Marshal General for the Union Army of the Potomac. At this point he had been performing the same function for all of the Federal armies operating against Richmond.
14. There are a few variations in the wording presented on April 27th and 28th, which seem of minor consequence, but which excited the interest of the Councilmen who would state them as an official resolution of defeated Southerners.
15. Colonel E.V. Sumner had made his headquarters in the bank building that still stands at the corner of Princess Anne and George Streets (Fredericksburg Ledger, June 10, 1865).
16. Fredericksburg Ledger, May 23, 1865.
17. Francis H. Pierpont was a lawyer who had been instrumental in the revolt of 32 western Virginia counties who opposed their state seceding from the Union. He led them in setting up a government separate from the Richmond government, which led to their secession from the seceding Commonwealth of Virginia. The United States government admitted the state of West Virginia into the Union in 1863. During the war, Pierpont became the Provisional Governor of those portions of Virginia that were held by the Union army and he remained governor after the war had ended. His association with Union forces would not have endeared him to the former Confederates, but they refer to him as his excellency in the minutes. Perhaps the overwhelming number of Federal troops that had marched through town over a period of two weeks had sent a strong message that the South had lost its war. Ironically, the Radical Republicans in the U.S. Congress did not consider Pierpont to be hard enough for the proper Reconstruction of Virginia and he was forced from office in 1868. The obstructions in the river consisted of numerous sunken vessels.

18. Thomas Mealy Harris had commanded combat troops in the 24th Corps, Army of the James.
19. The Fredericksburg and Gordonsville Rail Road Company had begun work to construct a railway in 1853. By the time of the Civil War, 18 miles had been graded to the west and this cleared route was referred to as the unfinished railroad on three battlefields—Fredericksburg, Chancellorsville, and the Wilderness. After the war, construction did not resume until 1873.
20. The tax rates adopted by the Town Council on August 8, 1865 clearly met with significant local opposition and they had to adopt revised tax rates on August 21st that cut most of the proposed taxes in half. The need for revenue to rebuild the community confronted people's ability to pay such taxes. The taxes appear to have fallen more heavily on working class persons, while professionals such as doctors and attorneys had very light taxes placed on their business licenses. The professional class citizens also likely paid higher property taxes, but there still appears to have been an unfair disparity in how taxes were levied.
21. Hart & Hayes was a store in the 300 block of William Street that became the distribution point for food received for destitute citizens. It is referenced in the Fredericksburg Ledger, July 24, 1865. The building is no longer extant.
22. Andrew Johnson had been governor of Tennessee until elected to the U.S. Senate in 1856. He had been an ardent Unionist was elected as Lincoln's vice president in 1864 and had become President when Lincoln was shot in April 1865. See Note 17 for details on Governmor Pierpont.
23. Samuel Sprigg Carroll, West Point class of 1856, was a veteran of the campaigns fought in Virginia. He had lost his left arm at Spotsylvania Court House.
24. The graveyard on Prince Edward Street was known as the Corporation Burying Ground and the brick wall surrounding it had fallen into disrepair. Burials had ceased before the Civil War, but animals were apparently finding their way in. This cemetery was cleared of bodies in the 1870s and converted to a park in 1881. The park was named after John G. Hurkamp, local businessman and member of the Town Council.

25. The railway bridge at Fredericksburg had been burned in 1862, but its stone abutments remained intact. After the war, the Richmond, Fredericksburg & Potomac Railroad hired former Confederate Major E.T.D. Myers as their engineer to rebuild it. Myers constructed a wooden structure on the existing stone abutments. In 1882, the R.F.&P. replaced the wooden bridge with an iron one and replaced that with a steel bridge in 1889. All of these structures were for a single track. A double track bridge was not built until 1926-27. It is a poured concrete structure, built just upstream of the Civil War bridge and it remains in use today. The issues related to the tracks through town were handled by another engineer, Colonel Carter M. Braxton.

26. The Bureau for the Relief of Refugees and Freedmen had been established by the U.S. Congress in March of 1865 and Major General Oliver Otis Howard became its commissioner in May of that year. The Freedmen's Bureau tried to help freed slaves transition to wage labor, contracts, and life outside of bondage, but the Southern economy desperately needed black labor and did not typically appreciate the interference of the Federal agency. An example of some of the Freedmen's Bureau's work is an extremely rare register of formerly enslaved persons for Caroline County, for which the CVBT published an index of the names therein (Fredericksburg History and Biography, 2005).

27. Fredericksburg's mill races were critical to local industries. In the devastation that followed the Civil War, waterpower held promise for rebuilding the wrecked economy.

28. The Rappahannock River had been blocked with sunken vessels, which needed to be cleared if the waterway was going to be returned to commercial use.

29. M.A. stood for Mutual Assurance, an insurance company.

Southern Exposure
Aerial Photo of the Fredericksburg Battlefield.

BY ERIK F. NELSON

The terrain south of Fredericksburg takes on the characteristics of the relatively flat and open ground of the Virginia Tidewater region. Both Union and Confederate forces maneuvering there found few advantages once they moved beyond the cover of their own artillery. The Union army placed its batteries of guns along a series of hills on the north side of the Rappahannock River, effectively covering engineer units and infantry regiments engaged in establishing a bridgehead downstream from Fredericksburg. Such crossings occurred in December 1862, in April 1863, and again in June of that year. Confederates who tried to hinder construction of the pontoon bridges were constrained from moving up artillery, which would have been destroyed by the better positioned Federal guns. As a consequence, only infantry could be positioned along the river and invariably found itself very vulnerable. The foot soldiers could provide a token resistance, but always needed to fall back from that exposed position in the face of superior fire power that attended any concerted advance.

Once the Federals crossed, however, it was they who were at a disadvantage. Infantry needed to move forward across the flat and open ground toward a series of hills from which Confederate artillery could blast them. There was some cover to be found along the Richmond Stage Road, also called the Bowling Green Road. At various times, this road embankment sheltered advanced pickets as well as main lines of battle. Beyond the road is more open ground, which rises slightly roughly midway between the road and a railway. This terrain feature bisects the ground recently preserved as the Slaughter Pen. Federal field artillery could also be advanced to the road to support its infantry.

In 1933, the U.S. Army Air Corps took the photograph shown here. Aviation had made an appearance on the battlefield during the First World War and the armed forces of the world had since been developing their respective air arms with an eye toward a future conflict, which did not appear to be too distant. This photograph would have been taken by an observation squadron, separate from bomber or pursuit (fighter) squadrons.

Between the world wars, the U.S. Army wrestled with the issue of how best to integrate an air arm into organizations established before men could fly. Between 1926 and the beginning of World War II, Army doctrine was to use its aircraft in direct support of ground forces. This photo illustrates a growing reconnaissance capability, in an area where balloons had been used during the Civil War. There was a strong faction within the Army Air Corps that saw an air force becoming an independent arm in its own right, but that reality lay in the future.

This view taken in 1933 is looking down the Rappahannock River, with Fredericksburg on the right and Stafford County on the left. The photo made its way into the local Historic and Business Guide for Fredericksburg of that year, which pointed out the new railway bridge (second bridge from the bottom), just upstream from where the Civil War era railway bridge had stood. The Guide also noted George Washington's boyhood home, just downstream of the railway bridge, on the Stafford side of the river.

Civil War landmarks include Chatham, in the lower left of the photo. The open area on the opposite shore, three blocks upstream of the metal frame bridge, is the upper pontoon crossing site, used in December 1862 and again in May 1863. The middle pontoon crossing was located just downstream of the railway bridge and the lower crossing occurred still further downstream, where the river bends to the left. The related pontoon bridges at this lower crossing spanned the river at the farthest point to the left of this bend.

As has been noted, the terrain is flat and open. The Richmond Stage Road (Bowling Green Road) and the low ridge across the Slaughter Pen roughly parallel the river. A stream called Deep Run, however, cuts across this terrain and provided a way for forces to move across this ground with some protection. Deep Run is visible as the line of trees that extends from the river toward the Confederate position on the right. In December 1862, the Vermont brigade took advantage of its cover as did many other units trying to get closer to their adversary.

On December 13, 1863, the Federals moved across the open ground to the Richmond Stage Road and attacked the line of hills on the other side of the Slaughter Pen. In late April and early May 1863, during the Chancellorsville campaign, Confederate forces held the Richmond Stage Road until the evening of May 2nd, when they were pulled back (mistakenly it turned out) and the Federals, who had established a bridgehead on April 29th, advanced into the vacuum. On May 3rd, Union forces used the cover of Deep Run to move up from the road toward the Confederate line. As fighting intensified during this Deep Run advance, the main Federal assault on Marye's Heights overran the Confederate position and that stunning success caused all of the engaged units at Deep Run to pull back and respond to the new developments.

In November of 2013, the historians at the Fredericksburg and Spotsylvania National Military Park presented this photo on their blog site, *Mysteries and Conundrums*. It can be viewed there in an interactive mode that allows one to zoom in to specific points. A full 70 years had passed between the Civil War action in this area and the time of the photograph, but much of the landscape remains as it looked in 1862-1863. Federal observation balloons had been used in this area, but no photographers are known to have made an ascent. This photograph suggests what those early aeronauts might have seen, although they were admittedly at a much lower altitude.

Index

A

Abbot, Peter 10
Adams, Robert B. 50
Adams, Robert W. 150-152, 158-159, 163-164
Aler, A.C. 123
Aler, Ann E. 134
Aler, George 113
Alexander, J.H. 117
Alexander, R.H. 113
Allen, J. William 46, 51
Allen, Jeremiah 150
Allen, John W. E. 46, 51
Allen, Jos. A. 49
Ames, Michael 113
Andrews, John L. 104
Armat, C. 107
Armstrong, Alexander 113
Armstrong, William K. 52
Armstrong, William R. 44
Averitt, Eliza 67

B

Ball, Joseph 45, 53
Bandy, William A. 52
Barton, Thomas B. 109, 124-125, 127, 129, 161, 163
Baugh, John, F. 52
Baughan 48, 52
Bawl, Joseph J. 53
Beamm, S.H. 49, 54
Bender, Frank J. 53
Bender, J.E. 46, 53
Bernard, Arthur 13, 28
Berry, John J. 110, 156, 158
Blackstone, B.C. 49

Bland, John L. 47, 54
Blann, Stephen H. 54
Bode, August 54
Bohannan, John A. 48, 55
Bondis, A. 47, 56
Boon, Nathan S. 55
Born, N. 49, 55
Bradley, James H. 104, 106-109, 111, 114, 117-122, 129, 159
Bradshaw, John 45, 55
Bradshaw, Walter 113
Brandon, William S. 47, 56
Brandy, Y.B. 44, 52
Brannan, William 113
Braxton, Carter M. 141, 154, 168n
Broaddus A. Thomas 56
Brode, A. 47, 54
Brooks, William T.H. 11, 13, 14, 23
Buck, Erastus 12, 24
Budd, Joseph H. 46, 56
Bull, Frederick 57
Bull, John 57
Bullock, John A. 44, 57
Burke, William 113, 143
Burnside, Ambrose E. 10, 30
Burr, Peter P. 107, 133
Burton, John L. 43, 50, 57
Bush, Henry 20
Buttery, Jordan L. 58
Butting, Joseph 47, 58

C
Cage, William L. 47, 58
Calwell, William C. 58
Carrell, Benjamin F. 113
Carroll, Samuel Spriggs 152, 168n
Carter, Edward 133
Carter, Walter 45, 59

Carter, William 59
Cash, Charles 113
Cathon, B. 44, 63
Causey, Alfred E. 59
Chew, George F. 105, 108, 124, 130, 133, 140-142
Chew, John J. 113
Chewning, Francis B. 113
Christian, E.G. 46, 59
Christian, N. H. 59
Clark, B. 119
Clark, J.B. 45, 47
Clark, J.C. 49, 60
Clark, James 23, 29
Clark, Judson 17
Clarke, Noah 47, 61
Clarke, Thomas B. 61
Clarkson, Jno. M. 106
Clengan, D.A. 44, 61
Clingan Davis Alexander 61
Coakley, John 124, 126
Cole, Counseller 112
Coleman, T. F. 50, 61
Coleman, Thomas T. 113
Collins, Finley 44, 62
Colwell, William 45, 58
Conway, W.P. 143
Corbett, Richard 62
Corbit, Richard 45, 62
Cosser, A.E. 46, 59
Cothran, Benjamin F. 63
Covington 117
Cox, Abraham 113
Cox, James E. 46, 63
Cox, William 113
Cummings, W. T. 46, 63

Cunningham, William H. 104, 106-108, 114-115, 119, 121-125, 127-138, 140-142, 144-146, 150-153, 155-156, 158-161, 163-164
Curtis, Samuel D. 113

D
Dabney, John W. 44, 64
Daily, James A. 64
Dale, Evans 45, 64
Daller, William 44, 65
Daly, J.A. 49, 64
Damson, John C. 45
Davidson, Greenlee 33n
Davis, Jefferson 103
Davis, Lauchlin 46, 64
Dawson, John C. 65
Day, Redrick M. 49, 65
Dodd, Ira 19
Doggett, Hugh S. 157
Dollar, Willliam 65
Dowell, James R. 150
Dubois, Charles 22-25
Duvall, Daniel A. 46, 66

E
Edwards, Reuben. J. 45, 66
Elder, John D. 113
Eldridge 49, 66
Elridge, I. W. 66
Emery, Edson 30
Evans, David L. 49, 67
Evans, John T. 113
Eve, George W. 105, 107-110, 113, 120-122, 124-134
Everett, Robert 47, 67

F
Fairbanks, Erastus 31n
Farr S. John 44, 68

Farrs, John 44, 68
Ficklen, James B. 158-159
Fitzgerald, George 47, 68
Fitzhugh, Anne 42
Ford, Kelly Tackett 105
Foster, George P. 19(photo), 25
Foster, James H. 49, 68
French, Walter Y. 45, 69

G
Gaddy, Clem 69
Gaddy, Rachel M. 69
Gardiner, Cosley W. 69
Gardner, Cosley 47, 69
Gardner, M.M. 117
Gatewood, George 70
Gatewood, John Dudley 48, 70
Gatewood, William 46, 70
Gerrell, A.F. 70
Gibbon, John 19-22
Gill, Beverly T. 107-110, 114-115, 117-121, 123-125, 127-142, 144-146, 150, 153, 156, 159-161, 163-164
Gillman, George 107
Gillman, William S. 129
Goolrick, Charles T. 158
Gordon, D.H. 105-106
Gordon, G.W. 163
Grant, Lewis A. cover(photo), 11, 21-22, 25-26, 29-30
Gravatt, George 106-107, 126-127, 129, 131-138, 140-142, 145-146, 153, 155-157, 160-161, 163-164
Green, Edward 71
Green, Joseph 47, 71
Greer, Edward 47, 71
Greer, Joseph 71
Griffin, Levi 45, 71
Grinnell, D. 46, 70

H

Hack, Lester 26
Hall, Horace B. 106-108, 110-111, 114-115, 117-121, 123, 125-138, 140-141, 145-146, 150
Hall, Joseph 114
Hammack 120
Handison, J.C. 44, 73
Hanes, James K. 72
Harden, S.L. 49, 72
Hardin, Samuel L. 72
Harrell, Edward 45, 72
Harrer, J. 45, 72
Harris, Thomas Mealy 142, 167n
Harrison, Lee 42
Harrison S.C. 73
Hart, Robert W. 108, 123, 132-134, 141, 151, 156
Hayes, James 151
Hayes, Jas. H. 73
Heath, Joseph H. 44, 73
Heinichen, Edward L. 110-111, 143, 164n
Henderson, James B. 45, 73
Henry, Isaac F. 74
Henry, John G. 74
Henry, T.F. 44, 74
Henry, Thomas J. 74
Henry, William 105
Herbert, M.M. 49, 75
Herndon, Charles 133-146, 150-153, 155-157, 159, 163
Herndon, John M. 105, 107-108, 121, 126-127
Hicks, Stephen L. 44, 74
Higgen, Newton 48, 74
Higgins, Newton 74
Hill, W.H. 143
Holloway, N. A. 46, 75
Hooe, Richardetta Mason 166n
Howard, Oliver Otis 168n
Howe, Albion 10, 13-15, 17, 22, 25-27, 29

Hubbard, Josiah 46, 75
Hubbert M.M. 75
Hudson, Richard 113
Huffman, Landon J. 108-109, 113, 133, 143
Humphreys, Charles 119
Hurkamp, John G. 104, 106-107, 109-111, 113, 117-119, 121, 123-125,
    128-129, 132-142, 144, 151, 156-157, 159-161, 163-164, 165n, 168n
Hyde, Breed N. 22 (photo), 23, 25, 29

J

Jarrell, A.F. 70
Jarrell, James 75
Jeffries, William J. 105
Jerrold, James 46
Johnson, Andrew 152, 168n
Johnson, William Howell 44, 76
Johnston, Gabriel 113
Johnston, Wyatt 114
Joice, George W. 76
Joice, John 113
Jones, James B. 156
Jones, William W. 114
Joyce, Charles H. 17 (photo), 25, 29
Joyce, George W. 47, 76

K

Kendall, James T. 106, 108, 118-119, 132, 134
Kewell, C.S. 156
King, George P. 123
Knight, John L. 109, 113, 122
Knox, Thomas F. 112, 133-141, 150, 152, 159, 164

L

Lackey, Edward 76
Lackey, William 46, 77
Lango, William 114
Latimer, Joseph 33n

Law, Evander M. 23-25
Laymon, William P. 45, 77
Layton, Lewis 141
Leach, Chester K. 29
Leach, W.K. 46, 77
Lee, Robert E. 10, 130
Leech, William H.H. 77
Letterman, Jonathan 28
Letty, Edward 45, 76
Lewis, Francis P. 47, 78
Little, A.A. 162
Little, William A. 104, 106-111, 114-143, 145-146, 149-150, 152-153, 157-158, 161
Liverman, Frederick 47, 78
Lord, Nathan 15(photo), 26, 30
Love, Lucien 113
Luster, Morgan 44, 78
Lynch, Henry N. 45, 79
Lynch, William C. 44, 79

M

Mander, Charles 113
Manuell, Thomas 114
Marbang Sevear 47, 79
Marbury, Sevier 80
Marchman, Stephen R. 44, 80
Martin, Leonard 15, 21, 26
Marye, James B. 113
Marye, John L., Jr. 163
Mashburn John 80
Mashman, J. 45, 48
Mazeen, James 113
McAdams, James O.A. 81
McCance, Robert 46, 81
McCartney, William 17, 23-24
McCrey, David 49, 82
McDowell, E. 152

McDowell, Patrick 113
McGuire, James 104, 107-112, 114-115, 118-119, 121-125, 128, 131-142, 144-146, 150-153, 156-161, 163-164
McKee 50, 81
McKie, William 81
McRae, David B. 82
McRoberts, Joseph 82
McRoberts, Robert 44, 82
Meade, George Gordon 139
Mellish, George 27
Miller, Ezekiel P. 49, 82
Miller, Joseph A. 50, 83
Miller, M.T. 82
Miller, William T. 82
Mills, Walter M. 113
Millsaps, Duncan G.C. 46, 83
Minor, John 113
Moore, Horace 44, 83
Moore, Lewis 113
Morse, W.R. 161
Mose 45, 83
Moss, William 83
Moulbry, Sev. 47, 80
Mullen, George 113, 122, 133
Murphy, Thomas 30
Myer, Fred 44
Myers, E.T.D. 168n
Myers, Felix 84

N
Neil, Thomas H. 25
Newton, John 13-14, 27
Newton, Thomas 113
Newton, Wellinghly 120-122
Norton, William H. 51, 59, 70, 76-77, 81
Nye, Cornelius 17

O

O'Donnell, Michael 45, 84
Old, John N. 84-85
Old, J.M. 50, 84
Oliver, Henry B. 85
Oliver, Henry P. 85
Oliver, John A. 49, 85
Oliver, N.P. 47, 85
Ould, R. 117
Overstreet, Christenbury C. 44, 86
Owen, J.T. 47, 86

P

Paddy, Clem 46, 69
Parker, Daniel A. J. 46, 86
Parker, Robert S. 113
Parr, John D. 68
Patrick, Marsena Rudolph 136, 138, 166n
Perry, Richard M. 49, 87
Peyton, Berry 163
Peyton, George H. 113
Pharr Samuel J. 68
Phillips, Alexandria K. 162
Phillips, Margaret 162
Pierpont, Francis H. 140, 152, 167n
Pingree, Samuel E. 22
Pingree, Stephen M. 20, 29
Pitridge, John 26
Pittman, Cannon 45, 87
Pitts, Richard C. 45, 87
Placer, John M. 44, 87
Placie, John M. 87
Pope, James A. 45, 88
Pope, John B. 45, 88
Powers, Henry M. 113
Pratt, Calvin E. 14-15
Pratt, Thomas 166n

Pratt, William 131, 166n
Pridgan 45, 88
Pridgers, Samuel 88

R

Read, James G. 107, 133, 135
Reinz, Christopher 113
Reynolds, John F. 14, 27
Reynolds, R.B. 113
Richardson, Israel B. 31n
Riffe, Joshua 44, 89
Roach, William H. 44, 89
Robinson, Samuel C. 44, 89
Rogers, J. Stewart 50, 90
Rose, Laurence B. 104, 107-108, 111, 115, 117-123, 125-127, 130
Rowe, G.H.C. 115, 116-119, 130, 145, 150
Ruggles, Daniel 129-130, 166n

S

Sacrey, George F. 113
Sager, T. 45, 90
Sample, E.A. 117
Samuel, Argalus E. 113, 151
Samuel, C.S. 48, 90
Sasser, Larkin P. 90
Saunders, Harrison S. 90
Sawyer, William J. 45, 91
Scott, Amanda B. 91
Scott, Benjamin F. 45, 91
Scott, Charles S. 133-146, 150-151, 153, 155-160, 163-164
Scott, John F. 109, 111-112, 114, 126, 130, 143, 153
Seaver, Thomas O. 22, 23 (photo), 24-25, 28-29
Seddon, James A. 111
Sener, Joseph W. 107-109, 113, 118-125, 127-130, 132-141, 143-146, 150-153, 155-164
Shackleford, James W. 50, 91
Shepherd, Gordon W. 49, 92

Sherman, William T. 11, 139
Slaughter, Montgomery 104-106, 108-112, 114-125, 127-145, 150-153, 155-157, 159-163
Smith, John H. 50, 92
Smith, Robert 113
Smith, William C. 113
Smith, William F. 10-14
Sneed, Alex 92
Snead, Alex. 47, 92
Solan, John 113
Southard, James 49, 93
Southerland, William J. 93
Spindle, W.W. 133
Stamess, Lawrence 46
Start, Storrs 17
Stedham, James M. 45, 94
Stephens, Edward W. 109, 133
Stephens, Eli E. 48, 93
Stephens, Martha 119, 129, 165n
Stevens, Samuel H. 46, 93
Stevens, William 20, 27, 30
Stewart, Lacy 49, 94
Stidham, Jobus M. 94
Stone, Edward P. 30
Stott, Addison D. 45, 94
Stoughton, Charles B. 19
Stowers, Charles 95
Stowers, Lawrence P. 95
Sumner, Edwin V. 102, 167n
Sutton, William 46, 95

T
Taylor, Buddy 151
Taylor, James A. 45, 95, 106, 108, 113, 141
Terry 152
Thomas, George H. 11
Thomas, William H. 113

Thornton, Thomas S. 113
Tilley, Edmund 46, 95
Tilley, Hiram 17
Timberlake, John S.G. 104, 114, 134, 141
Trenholm, George Alfred 126, 165n
Trots, Norton 45, 96
Trott, Newton 96
Trussle Joseph A. John 47, 96
Tubbs, Samuel 44, 96
Twitchell, Marshall 20-21

V

Vassar, John E. 156
Vaughan, Carter 46, 97
Vinton, Francis L. 14-15, 17, 19, 28

W

Waite, Charles B. 109, 113, 143, 151, 157
Waite, Charles G., Jr. 113
Walker, H. A. 46, 97
Wallace, J. Gordon 104, 106-107, 116, 120, 133
Warwick, B.B. 66
Webb, Wyatt B. 113
Weeks, S. S. 97
Wells, Henry H. 115, 165n
White, Albert W. 48, 98
White, William 113
Whiting, Henry 9, 10 (photo), 13-15, 17-18, 28-29
Wicks, S.S. 49, 97
Wilder, Reuben L.W. 44, 98
Williams, Charles 113
Williams, George W. 47, 99
Williams, Joseph G. 46, 98
Williams, Tandy 113
Willig, W.G. 48, 99
Wills, I.B. 99
Wiltshire, William 113

Witherspoon John G. 48, 99
Woodard, John D. 49, 100
Woodward, J.D. 100
Wootan Thomas J. 100
Wrenn, Lewis 113
Wright, W. 121
Wroten, George W. 47, 113, 134, 143
Wroten, Joseph T.J. 100
Wroten, Sarah W. 122

Y
Young, Jonathan James 106-111, 114-115, 117-119, 121, 123, 125-130, 132-138, 140-142, 144, 150-153, 156-157, 160, 163-164
Young, Nathan M. 44, 100